FAST FOOD
for BUSY FAMILIES

This book is dedicated to all the families who are on the path to improved health and wellness. No matter where you are on your journey, every step forward is a step in the right direction to great health. Our children are the future, so let's ensure they have the very best nutritional foundation to lead our country back to optimal health. Together we have the power to make a massive change.

FAST FOOD

for BUSY FAMILIES

More than 100
quick & easy PALEO RECIPES

PETE EVANS

 plum. Pan Macmillan Australia

CONTENTS

Introduction 7
Ready, set, cook! 10
Handy equipment 12

Kids'
snacks in a
flash 48

Breakfast
in a flash
28

BREAKFASTS 15

KIDS' LUNCHES 43

Spreads &
dips in a
flash 58

SALADS 67

Salad
dressings &
toppings in a
flash 86

MAIN MEALS 125

SIDES 205

Barbecue
ideas in a
flash 142

Entertaining
in a flash
172

TREATS 223

BASICS 241

Warming
drinks in a
flash 230

Glossary 259
Thank you 265
Index 267

INTRODUCTION

Firstly, for those of you who are new to paleo, I want to thank you for having the courage to take the first steps to a long and healthy life. And for those of you who have been on this path for a while now, thank you for your commitment to this healthy lifestyle and for being part of a movement that is taking Australia and New Zealand by storm.

Over the last few years I have been so fortunate to travel and teach people the simple premise of living the paleo way – through our international stage shows, *The Paleo Way* television series, magazines, cookbooks and social media. We now have over 1 million Facebook followers and each and every day we share another remarkable story of someone who has transformed their life by following the paleo way principles. Each story brings a tear to my eye. So many of these people have lived with pain, lack of energy or low self esteem, and all it took were some simple changes to their diet and lifestyle for them to reclaim their health.

The paleo way has now definitely hit the mainstream, which is a great sign as it means that people are switching over to this lifestyle through word of mouth from friends and family. However, there is still a lot of misunderstanding about what a paleo lifestyle involves, so for those of you who are unsure or who are new to this way of living, let me explain it as simply as I can.

Eating the paleo way is about embracing real foods and eliminating any foods that may cause inflammation in our bodies. The most common culprits for this are gluten (and grains), legumes, dairy, toxic oils (such as seed and vegetable oils) and refined sugars. If you have an auto-immune issue, you may also consider eliminating nightshade vegetables (such as tomatoes, eggplants, capsicums and potatoes), nuts and eggs for a period of time too to see how that impacts your health.

So what foods do we embrace? You'll be pleased to know that there is an abundance of natural and delicious foods to include in your diet. Here are our recommendations:

- Eat up to a palm-sized portion of animal protein at every meal. Focus on sourcing protein from animals that have had a natural diet, such as grass-fed beef, wild-caught seafood, free-range and pasture-raised poultry and pigs, and wild game.
- Enjoy an abundance of organic vegetables, with a preference for the least starchy varieties.

- Include good-quality fat from avocados, olives, nuts, seeds, eggs and animals in your daily diet.
- Include bone broth in your daily diet for good gut health. You can drink bone broth straight up, or add it to soups, curries or braises.
- Add a spoon of fermented vegetables to every meal if possible. Start off with a teaspoon a day, then work your way up to about a tablespoon or two per meal.

As with any dietary changes, always consult your health professional and inform them of your intentions to make sure they feel it is safe for you, taking into account your overall health and any medical conditions that you may have. Luckily, more and more doctors are promoting this way of life for their patients, which is wonderful to see.

So, why this book? Well, it is a result of listening to you. As I mentioned before, I love meeting, talking and connecting with people all over the world, and the thing that I most often get asked for help with is quick and simple paleo recipes that the whole family will love. We all live extremely busy lives and most of us need to put food on the table seven nights a week. When we are in a rush and feeling stressed, we need nourishing meals that can be made in less than an hour. When first transitioning to a paleo way of eating, it's often easier to start with cooking paleo versions of meals that are familiar family favourites. So, I have channelled my 25 years of experience as a chef into creating paleo versions of spaghetti and meatballs, burgers, rolls, roasts, curries, breakfast cereals and desserts, because these are the dishes that kids especially are comfortable with and ones that will get requested again and again. I love it when I hear from a reader that their family enjoyed one of my paleo recipes so much that they now cook it every single week. I love it even more when I hear that these recipes have transformed their children's relationship to mealtime and that meals are once again a joyous occasion.

I have also included some offal dishes to take you out of your comfort zone! This incredibly nutrient-dense food is something that many Western people steer clear of, which I think is a real shame. If you are not fond of offal I have offered alternatives, but I also encourage you to challenge yourself to eat something new from time to time. Check out the crumbed chicken liver nuggets on page 60 to see what I mean about people discovering the pleasure of something they thought was icky!

With this book, I want to show you that paleo does not have to be difficult. It can be as simple as a piece of pan-fried fish with a salad, a roast with veggies or a bowl of chicken and vegetable soup. But there are also many other ways you can save time in the kitchen and make cooking a whole lot easier for yourself. My number one piece of advice is to invest in a chest freezer if you have the space, so that you can store leftover meals. Buy a heap of containers, then double or triple the recipes and freeze them for another time. If you have healthy food on hand you are less likely to make poor food choices. And you'll also have more time to spend with your family and friends doing the things you love.

I also recommend shopping locally and seasonally whenever you can. Cultivate a relationship with local farmers, greengrocers and butchers. When you first start out, try to write a meal plan at the start of every week. Do most of your shopping at the weekend if possible, ensure your cupboards and fridge are well stocked with healthy produce and ingredients, and cook up basics like paleo bread, cereal and bone broth on the weekend so that you can use them to create quick meals throughout the week. See pages 10–13 for more tips on how to save time in the kitchen.

I also encourage you to read more on paleo as I think that the more people understand the science behind this way of eating, the more motivated they are to continue to make wise food choices. My dear friend Nora Gedgaudas's book, *Primal Body, Primal Mind*, is a great place to start. As Nora says when she speaks about paleo: 'We are not extreme, merely informed'.

This book is broken up into chapters – which I encourage you to pay no notice to! At the end of the day, no-one needs to be told what to eat for breakfast, lunch or dinner, and I want you to break the rules. Try some of the breakfast ideas for dinner and have leftovers of your dinner for breakfast or lunch the next day. The only thing I will say is to view the recipes in the treats chapter as ones to enjoy very occasionally. Sugar is sugar, whether it is honey or refined white sugar, and if you spike your blood sugar level too much and too often then problems will manifest. I have also included 'In a Flash' spreads with super quick ideas for breakfast, entertaining, kids' snacks, salad dressings and more. Please view all of my recipes as a guide only. If you are not confident then it's probably easier to follow the recipe exactly the first time you cook it. The next time, though, try to play around with it by using a different spice or herb, or swapping meat for fish or chicken. There is nothing I love more than when people post images of their food and say that they have changed my recipe, as it means they are getting creative and putting love into their cooking.

I hope you and your family enjoy cooking and eating this food as much as I do – I have no doubt that it will leave you feeling satisfied and full of energy. Please stay in touch through social media and let me know about your paleo way journey!

Keep cooking with love and laughter.

Pete xo

Ready, set, cook!

Cooking healthy, nourishing meals that will sustain you and your family does not have to take a huge amount of time. It's simply a matter of getting organised, having the right equipment and making the best use of the time that you do have. Here are my top tips for getting a delicious meal on the table in record time.

Plan your week

Take the stress out of weeknight dinners by making a loose plan of what you are going to eat for dinner each night of the week. Head to a market on the weekend and buy everything you'll need for your meals for the week. This way, you won't have to worry about squeezing in a trip to the shops in between work and home, and you'll have more time on weeknights to relax and enjoy eating with your family.

Double your quantities

Whenever possible, make up double or even triple batches of recipes – especially ones that freeze well. Of course, this won't work for fresh salads or ceviche, but there are loads of recipes in this book that are perfect for storing in the fridge or freezer and enjoying later. My lunches these days are almost always delicious leftovers from the night before. The meatball sauce from spaghetti and meatballs (page 200) freezes really well, the snapper curry with roasted cauliflower and okra (page 166) is even better the next day and leftover Indian-style roast chicken drumsticks (page 174) make a brilliant snack.

Cook up a storm on the weekends Weekends are the perfect time to make all of those things that take a little bit longer, like paleo bread (page 257), burger buns (page 248), bone broth (page 254), superfood 'cereal' (page 18), nut milk (page 16) and dips or sauces (see Basics chapter). If you spend a few hours on the weekend prepping these basics, your week is going to flow so much more smoothly. I also usually cook up a big roast on the weekend, making sure I have leftover protein and roasted veg that I can use for breakfasts and lunches throughout the week.

Organise your kitchen

Having an organised kitchen will make it so much easier to prepare and cook meals quickly. Clear out your utensil drawer and cupboards and take any equipment you don't actually use to the op shop. You might like to keep the utensils that you use most often, like the whisk, spatula, wooden spoon and tongs, in a jar next to the stove so that you can reach them easily while cooking.

Embrace seafood

Seafood is nature's own 'fast food' and is delicious both raw and cooked. I've included some of my favourite raw fish dishes in this book, as they are so fast to prepare and make an impressive dinner for when friends come over – try my ceviche with pomegranate and mango (page 102) or Japanese tuna salad (page 95). Seafood also takes very little time to cook compared to many meat dishes, so make sure you check out the Main Meals chapter to find heaps of quick and tasty recipe ideas.

Invest in the right equipment

There's no need to spend a huge amount of money on equipment; however, there are a few essential pieces that will save you a whole lot of time in the long run that you could consider investing in. See over the page for my favourite pieces of equipment – ones that I use every week (or even every day) and that make me so much more efficient in the kitchen.

Handy equipment

BARBECUE

I love cooking on the barbecue – not only is it a really fast way to prepare meals, it also adds a delicious smoky taste to your food. There are lots of compact barbecues available these days, so even if you only have a small outdoors area you can still enjoy the great Australian traditional of throwing some meat on the barbie. For some quick ideas for barbecue meals, see pages 142–143.

Food processor

The right food processor can save you hours of chopping, slicing, mixing and grating. It is important to consider your needs before you invest in a food processor as size, quality and attachments vary greatly. I often use my food processor for making curry pastes and sauces.

Chargrill pan

A chargrill pan is an excellent tool when either weather or time doesn't allow for use of the barbie. Searing meat and vegetables in a chargrill pan gives them the characteristic black charring stripes, and as long as you heat the pan so that it's smoking hot, whatever you put on it will cook really quickly.

Jars, whisks and spatulas

All of these small utensils can really save you time in the kitchen. Hang on to small glass jars and use them to make salad dressings in a flash. Keep your whisks, ladles, slotted spoons and spatulas within easy reach – ideally near the stove top.

Heavy chopping board and sharp knives

Having a heavy chopping board and a good set of sharp knives will make your time in the kitchen more efficient and enjoyable. Make sure you look after your knives well and get them sharpened regularly.

HIGH-SPEED BLENDER

This is a great tool for quickly whipping up dips, sauces, nut milk and cashew cheese, to name a few. A good-quality high-speed blender will create finer pastes and smoother sauces than a food processor. Blenders vary greatly in quality so it is a good idea to research which blender suits your needs before you buy it – if you want to make nut butters regularly, for example, you probably want to buy quite a powerful blender.

Salad spinner

Washing and drying your leaves well is one of the keys to a delicious salad. You can dry salad leaves using clean tea towels, but a salad spinner will do the job much more quickly, and will mean you never have a soggy salad again.

MANDOLINE AND JULIENNE PEELER

Mandolines and julienne peelers are cheap and easy tools to save time while cooking, especially if your knife skills aren't great. Mandolines can slice vegetables super finely (and really quickly) and some of them also come with blades that julienne. Julienne peelers look similar to a regular vegetable peeler and are great for quickly julienning vegetables like carrot and cucumber for a salad.

Vegetable spiraliser

This tool is great for making vegetable pasta that the whole family will love. You can create spiral noodles from most vegetables – some of my favourites include zucchini, parsnip and beetroot.

Start your day
with nourishing
bone broth

UP AND AT
'EM!

Eat dinner for brekkie!

BREAKFASTS

ENJOY EGGS AND VEGGIES!

Greens
Fats
Nuts
Berries
Seeds

PREP:
6 mins (+ 5 mins for
macadamia milk &
8 hrs to soak)
COOK:
18 mins

Having a cup of the delicious ancient Ayurvedic drink golden mylk every day is a nourishing way to add more of the wonder spice turmeric to your diet. Turmeric's many healing benefits and vibrant golden colour come from its key active ingredient curcumin, a powerful antioxidant and anti-inflammatory. I like to have this hot in the cooler months and chilled or frozen into popsicles – the kids adore them – when it's warmer. In the recipe I strain out the nuts; however, you can also blend them into the milk to make a thicker and creamier drink.

SUNSHINE MYLK

1½ teaspoons coconut oil
5 cardamom pods, crushed
1 teaspoon Turmeric Paste
 (see below)
500 ml (2 cups) Macadamia Milk
 (see below) or coconut milk or
 coconut cream
pinch of freshly ground
 black pepper
¼ teaspoon vanilla powder
1 teaspoon honey or maple syrup
 (optional)
ground cinnamon, to serve

Macadamia milk
160 g (1 cup) macadamia nuts

Turmeric paste
4 tablespoons ground turmeric

If you'd like to use macadamia milk rather than coconut milk or cream, place the macadamia nuts in a bowl, cover with 1 litre of filtered water and soak for 8 hours or overnight. Drain and rinse well. Place the nuts in a high-powered blender with 1 litre of filtered water and blend until smooth. Line a bowl with a piece of muslin so that the muslin hangs over the edges of the bowl (alternatively you can use a nut milk bag). Pick up the edges of the muslin, bring together and twist to squeeze out all of the milk. (The leftover solids can be used to make bliss balls or in place of almond meal in baking recipes.) Pour the nut milk into a sterilised 1 litre bottle or jar, then refrigerate until ready to use. Shake the bottle before use as the milk will settle and separate after time.

Next, make the turmeric paste. Place the turmeric in a small saucepan with 250 ml of water. Simmer over low heat, stirring occasionally, until you have a creamy and smooth paste, about 15 minutes.

Place the coconut oil and cardamom in a saucepan and cook over medium–high heat until fragrant, about 1 minute. Reduce the heat to medium, add the remaining ingredients and stir for a few minutes until warmed through. Strain through a fine sieve.

Pour into glasses or mugs and enjoy with a sprinkle of cinnamon on top. (The leftover nut milk will keep in the fridge for 3–4 days; the leftover turmeric paste will keep for 2–3 weeks stored in an airtight glass container in the fridge.)

Serves 2

PREP:
8 mins
cook:
nil

Like most Aussie kids, I began every day with a bowl of cereal topped with milk. I also had recurring health problems – tonsillitis, a runny nose and an upset tummy. Unfortunately, these problems were never linked to the food I consumed. Luckily, we now have much more information about how food affects us, both positively and negatively. This delicious cereal has the snap, crackle and pop that a lot of kids, young and old, are accustomed to, without any of the nasties. Oh, and try topping it with some sunshine mylk (page 16), which is full of healing spices.

SUPERFOOD 'CEREAL'

2 tablespoons cacao nibs*
60 g (1 cup) coconut flakes
4 tablespoons chia seeds*
2 tablespoons flaxseeds*
80 g (½ cup) activated
  macadamia nuts, chopped
80 g (½ cup) activated almonds,
  toasted and chopped
80 g (⅔ cup) activated pecans,
  toasted and chopped
80 g (scant ⅔ cup) activated
  pumpkin seeds, toasted
4 tablespoons hulled hemp
  seeds*
1 teaspoon ground cinnamon
large pinch of vanilla powder

To serve
almond milk
fresh berries
honey (optional)

* See Glossary

Combine the cacao nibs, coconut flakes, chia seeds, flaxseeds, macadamias, almonds, pecans, pumpkin seeds, hemp seeds, cinnamon and vanilla powder in a bowl.

Serve with almond milk, berries and a drizzle of honey, if desired.

Serves 6

TIP
Make up a double or triple batch so that you always have a quick and healthy breakfast when you're in a hurry. Store in an airtight container in the cupboard.

Paleo is all about abundance and enjoyment and using foods that don't cause inflammation in our bodies (and minds). I find a lot of people who start on the paleo journey have the best results when their favourite foods are reinterpreted or adapted. Many people start their day with a traditional bircher muesli based on oats. In this bircher recipe, a sure-fire winner, I swap the oats for nutritionally dense chia seeds. I hope you and the whole family like it.

PREP:
10 mins (+8 hrs to soak)
COOK:
nil

CHIA BIRCHER

Place the chia seeds, flaxseeds, shredded coconut, coconut yoghurt, almond milk and apple in a bowl and mix to combine. Cover with plastic wrap and refrigerate for 8 hours or overnight. If the chia bircher is a little dry after soaking, stir through some more almond milk.

Spoon the bircher into serving bowls and top with the goji berries, almonds, yoghurt and fruit. Add a sprinkle of hemp seeds and a drizzle of honey, if desired.

Serves 3–4

80 g (½ cup) chia seeds*
3 tablespoons flaxseeds*
3 tablespoons shredded coconut
250 g (1 cup) coconut yoghurt
400 ml almond milk (plus extra
   if needed)
1 green apple, grated

To serve
goji berries*, soaked in water for
   10 minutes to soften
chopped activated almonds
coconut yoghurt
fresh fruit (such as sliced pear
   and figs or berries)
hemp seeds (optional)
honey (optional)

* See Glossary

PREP:
15 mins
(+ 10 mins for bread)
COOK:
5 mins
(+1 hr 20 mins for bread)

Scrambled eggs are a wonderful quick meal to whip up for breakfast (or for any time of the day really). I wanted to include zucchini in quite a few recipes in this book, as anyone who grows their own veg knows that when summer comes around the zucchini harvest is abundant! I am also a huge fan of adding greens to your family's meals, especially at breakfast. My kids are used to starting their day with some zucchini, broccoli or leafy greens and I urge you to give it a whirl in your own kitchen. As with all savoury recipes, serve with a small amount of fermented vegetables on the side.

SCRAMBLED EGGS WITH ZUCCHINI SPAGHETTI AND RAISINS

4 eggs
2 tablespoons coconut cream or almond milk
2 tablespoons coconut oil or other good-quality fat*, melted
sea salt and freshly ground black pepper
½ avocado, finely diced
pinch of sumac*, to serve
baby mint leaves, to serve (optional)
4 thick slices of Nic's Paleo Bread (page 257), toasted

Zucchini spaghetti
1 tablespoon coconut oil or other good-quality fat*
1 large or 2 small zucchini, cut into spaghetti strips on a mandoline or julienne slicer
1 tablespoon chopped flat-leaf parsley
30 g (¼ cup) raisins
40 g (¼ cup) pine nuts, toasted

See Glossary

Whisk the eggs, coconut cream or almond milk and 1 tablespoon of oil or fat in a bowl, then season with salt and pepper.

Heat the remaining oil or fat in a non-stick frying pan over medium heat, pour in the egg mixture, add the avocado and, using a wooden spoon, lift and push from the outside to the centre of the pan until almost set, about 2 minutes. Remove from the heat, gently fold the mixture a few times and allow to stand for 1 minute, so that the residual heat finishes the cooking.

To make the spaghetti, heat the oil or fat in a frying pan over medium–high heat. Add the zucchini and parsley and sauté for 40 seconds, or until just beginning to soften. Season with salt and pepper, add the raisins and pine nuts and toss well. Continue to cook for 30 seconds, or until heated through.

Serve the spaghetti with the scrambled eggs, a sprinkle of sumac, some baby mint leaves (if using) and the toast on the side.

Serves 2

PREP:
2 mins
COOK:
15 mins
(+12–24 hours
for broth)

If there is one recipe in this book that I'd recommend people have every day it would be this ... or a version of it. The recipe here uses beef broth but you could substitute the beef bones for chicken, fish or any other bones you like. Bone broth is known for its amazing healing properties. For more information on the benefits of this wonder broth, please read *Gut and Psychology Syndrome* by Dr Natasha Campbell-McBride or *Nourishing Broth* by Sally Fallon. Either book will convince you to make bone broth part of your daily ritual.

NOURISHING BROTH WITH MARROW AND HERBS

1 × 8 cm piece of beef marrow bone, halved lengthways and knuckle removed (ask your butcher to do this)
sea salt and freshly ground black pepper
400 ml Beef Bone Broth (page 254)
pinch of ground turmeric
½ teaspoon grated ginger
1 teaspoon lemon juice, or to taste
1 teaspoon chopped flat-leaf parsley leaves

Preheat the oven to 220°C.

Place the marrow bones on a baking tray and season with salt and pepper. Roast for 15 minutes or until browned.

Gently warm the bone broth in a small saucepan over medium–low heat. Add the turmeric, ginger and lemon juice and season with some salt and pepper. Scrape out the marrow from the bone halves, roughly chop and add to the broth.

Pour the hot broth into a mug or serving bowl, scatter over the parsley and serve.

Serves 1

Quality mince with a decent fat content is one of my favourite ingredients. Not only is it super-economical and super-quick but from a flavour point of view nothing else comes close. If you have a good butcher, you can ask them to add some minced heart, liver or other offal to make the mince even more nutritionally dense. This simple recipe never fails to delight – if you have never had mince for breakfast, you have been missing out. Serve this with some Asian greens on the side or a simple cucumber salad and some fermented veg, of course.

PREP:
15 mins (+ 5 mins for zucchini or cauliflower rice)

COOK:
13 mins (+ 5 mins for zucchini or cauliflower rice)

THAI PORK MINCE WITH FRIED EGG

Heat a wok or large frying pan over medium–high heat. Add 1 tablespoon of oil or fat and swirl it around the pan. Crack the eggs into the pan and fry, shaking the pan gently to prevent the eggs from sticking, for 1–2 minutes, or until cooked to your liking. Lift out the eggs with a spatula, place on a plate and keep warm.

Return the pan to high heat, add the remaining oil or fat and the shallot and stir-fry for 30–40 seconds until softened. Stir in the garlic, ginger, beans and chilli and cook for 20 seconds until fragrant. Add the pork mince and stir-fry until brown, about 6 minutes.

Pour the stock or water into the pan and simmer for 2 minutes, then mix in the fish sauce and honey or coconut sugar. Toss through the basil and water spinach and, as soon as it has wilted (about 30 seconds), remove the pan from the heat. Season with salt and pepper.

Serve the mince topped with a warm fried egg and a sprinkle of coriander leaves, with lime wedges and cauliflower or zucchini rice on the side.

Serves 4

3 tablespoons coconut oil or other good-quality fat*
4 eggs
3 red Asian shallots, finely sliced
5 garlic cloves, finely chopped
1 teaspoon finely grated ginger
120 g green beans, sliced
1 long red chilli, deseeded and thinly sliced (leave the seeds in if you like it spicy)
600 g pork mince
4 tablespoons chicken stock or water
1½ tablespoons fish sauce
1 teaspoon honey or coconut sugar*
1 handful of Thai basil leaves
1 large handful of water spinach, chopped (see note)
sea salt and freshly ground black pepper
1 large handful of coriander leaves, chopped
lime wedges, to serve
Zucchini or Cauliflower Rice (page 208), to serve

See Glossary

Note

Water spinach is also known as morning glory. It is commonly used in Asian cuisine and is available from Asian grocers. If you can't find it, simply use any leafy greens that you have to hand.

Breakfast in a flash

In many parts of the world, soups and curries are standard breakfast fare. I know it's not the norm in Australia, but I reckon once you give it a go, there will be no turning back! Make up a big batch of any of the soups or curries in the main meals chapter and enjoy them the next morning for the quickest and tastiest brekkie.

Paleo bread (page 257) can be used in so many ways for a speedy and healthy breakfast. Try it with some smashed avocado, macadamia cheese (page 256) and a drizzle of extra-virgin olive oil. Add a couple of poached eggs if you have more time.

One of my favourite breakfasts requires only two ingredients. Simply soft-boil two eggs, pop them in egg cups, remove their tops and add a spoonful of salmon or trout roe to each. Yum!

Whenever you cook a roast, make sure there's enough for leftovers for breakfast the next day! Cut or shred the meat, then warm it in a frying pan or the oven. Toss the meat with some rocket leaves, tomato wedges and thinly sliced red onion, then drizzle with balsamic vinegar and olive oil. Serve with fried eggs on the side and some freshly cracked pepper over the top.

If you want to get fancy with your superfood 'cereal' (page 18) or chia bircher (page 21), serve them in glasses instead of bowls, layered with dollops of whipped coconut cream mixed with a pinch of vanilla powder and cinnamon. Top with fresh berries and mint leaves.

Make a simple frittata with leftover meat and veggies from the night before. Just whisk a few eggs in a bowl, shred your leftover meat, then add to the egg along with the veggies. Pour into a greased baking tray and bake in the oven until the eggs are set. Slice and eat! This is also great for lunches.

Scrambled eggs on toast is a classic breakfast dish and I love it on toasted paleo bread (page 257). Jazz it up by adding some smoked salmon and some rocket leaves dressed with a little olive oil and lemon juice on the side.

I am a huge fan of sausages, but not the usual supermarket ones that are filled with unimaginable things (fillers that cannot be considered real food). Traditionally, sausages were made from three things: animal fat, animal protein and spices. I was lucky enough to be in the deep south of the USA recently. Here I worked with the charismatic chef John Folse, a living legend, who taught me to make Andouille sausages, which are made with smoked pork. If you can't find Andouille sausages, any good-quality sausages will do. I have teamed the sausages with asparagus, eggs and tomatoes, but you can use whatever is in season.

ANDOUILLE SAUSAGES WITH POACHED EGGS AND ASPARAGUS

1 tablespoon apple cider vinegar
pinch of sea salt
4 eggs
2 bunches of asparagus, woody ends trimmed
1 tablespoon coconut oil or other good-quality fat*
8 × Andouille sausages or good-quality sausages of your choice
2 garlic cloves, finely chopped
freshly ground black pepper
12 cherry tomatoes, halved
12 yellow teardrop tomatoes, halved
8 basil leaves, torn
1 tablespoon balsamic vinegar or coconut aminos*
3 tablespoons extra-virgin olive oil

See Glossary

To poach the eggs, add the vinegar and salt to a saucepan of boiling water. Reduce the heat to medium–low so the water is just simmering. Crack an egg into a cup. Using a wooden spoon or whisk, stir the simmering water in one direction to form a whirlpool and drop the egg into the centre. Repeat with the three remaining eggs. Poach the eggs for 3 minutes, or until cooked to your liking. Using a slotted spoon, remove the eggs and drain on paper towel.

Meanwhile, cook the asparagus in boiling salted water until tender but still slightly crisp, about 1 minute. Drain, plunge into cold water to stop the cooking process, then drain again and set aside.

Heat the oil in a large frying pan over medium heat, add the sausages and cook for 10–12 minutes, tossing occasionally, until cooked through and golden brown. Remove from the pan and keep warm on a plate covered with foil, reserving the fat from the pan.

Return the pan to medium heat, add the asparagus and cook for 10 seconds. Add the garlic and some salt and pepper and cook for 1 minute, until it starts to turn golden.

Place the tomatoes, basil, balsamic vinegar or coconut aminos and olive oil in a bowl and toss. Season with salt and pepper.

Arrange the asparagus on serving plates, then place a poached egg on top. Place two sausages and some of the tomato salad on the side and finish with some pepper.

Serves 4

I love to create paleo recipes that reinterpret global classics. I couldn't think of a more delicious dish than this version of a Vietnamese pancake for a special breakfast. I first tried this when I travelled to Vietnam and it quickly became an all-time favourite. Here I have teamed it with prawns but feel free to use leftover roasted or poached chicken or pork, or even bacon. Once you try these beauties, breakfast will never be the same again. Serve with kimchi or other fermented veg on the side.

VIETNAMESE PANCAKES WITH PRAWN AND PORK SALAD

6 large eggs
250 ml (1 cup) almond milk or coconut milk
3 tablespoons coconut flour, sifted
2 teaspoons coconut oil, melted, plus extra for cooking
1 teaspoon ground turmeric
pinch of sea salt

Salad
2 tablespoons coconut oil
1 onion, cut into thin wedges
300 g pork mince
sea salt and freshly ground black pepper
200 g shelled and deveined raw prawns, roughly chopped
130 g bean sprouts
1 large handful of mixed Asian herbs (such as Vietnamese mint, coriander, Thai basil and mint leaves)

Nuoc cham
3 tablespoons fish sauce
3 tablespoons lime juice
1 teaspoon coconut sugar* (optional)
1 long red chilli, deseeded and finely chopped
1 garlic clove, finely chopped

* See Glossary

To make the nuoc cham, combine the fish sauce, lime juice, coconut sugar (if using), chilli, garlic and 1 tablespoon of water in a small bowl. Stir until the sugar dissolves. Set aside.

Whisk the eggs, almond or coconut milk, coconut flour, coconut oil, turmeric and salt in a bowl until well combined. Allow to stand for 10 minutes, then whisk again.

Meanwhile, start on the salad. Heat 1 tablespoon of oil in a 21 cm non-stick frying pan over high heat until just smoking. Add the onion and pork mince and stir-fry for 5 minutes until golden and cooked through. Season with salt and pepper and transfer to a plate, keeping warm. Wipe the pan clean and place over medium heat. Add the remaining oil and the prawn meat and cook, stirring occasionally, for 2–3 minutes until golden and cooked through. Season with a little salt and pepper and keep warm.

Lightly brush the same pan with some of the extra coconut oil and heat over medium–high heat. Add one-quarter of the pancake batter and tilt the pan, swirling the batter to cover the base and reach slightly up the sides. Cook for 2–3 minutes, or until the underside is lightly golden, then flip the pancake over and cook for a further 20 seconds. Transfer to a plate and cover with foil. Repeat with the remaining batter.

To finish the salad, combine the prawns, pork, bean sprouts and Asian herbs in a bowl. Pour in just enough nuoc cham to moisten the pork and prawns and toss well. Serve the pancakes topped with a large handful of the salad.

Serves 4

I have been paleo for over four years and the food I eat now has changed a great deal from the early days. Initially, I made lots of paleo bread, cookies and other baked goods; now I hardly go near any of that stuff. Instead I find myself excited about offal, fat, broths, fermented vegetables and drinks and an abundance of colourful vegetables. This breakfast dish really sums up where paleo is at for me: delicious fat in the form of bone marrow (roasted in the oven while I have a shower), served with eggs, fermented veggies and fresh herbs. If you don't have bone marrow, serve the eggs with avocado, bacon or even a piece of grilled fish.

PREP:
8 mins
COOK:
15 mins

SCRAMBLED EGGS WITH ROASTED BONE MARROW

Preheat the oven to 200°C.

Place the marrow bones on a baking tray and season with salt. Roast for 15 minutes, or until golden brown and cooked through.

Meanwhile, using a fork, whisk the eggs, coconut cream or almond milk and 1 tablespoon of oil or fat in a bowl, then season with salt and pepper.

Heat the remaining oil or fat in a non-stick frying pan over medium heat. Pour in the egg mixture and stir gently with a wooden spoon, lifting and pushing the egg mixture from the outside to the centre until the eggs are almost set, about 2 minutes. Remove from the heat, gently fold the mixture a few times and leave to stand for 30–60 seconds, allowing the residual heat to finish cooking the eggs.

Divide the scrambled eggs between serving plates and garnish with the chives, then add 2–3 pieces of roasted marrow bone sprinkled with pepper. Serve with the fermented vegetables and watercress on the side.

Serves 2

600 g centre-cut beef marrow bones, cut into 4 cm pieces, tendons trimmed (ask your butcher to do this)
sea salt and freshly ground black pepper
4 eggs
2 tablespoons coconut cream or almond milk
2 tablespoons coconut oil or other good-quality fat*, melted
4 chives, snipped into 2.5 cm lengths

To serve
fermented vegetables or sauerkraut
watercress leaves

* See Glossary

PREP:
10 mins
(+ 30 mins to soak &
5 mins for tapenade)

COOK:
14 mins

I am a huge fan of olives, whether they're green, black, fermented, dried or turned into tapenade, as in this recipe here. I love to find ways to incorporate them into our meals as often as possible and, to get the party started, often pop a small bowlful on the kitchen bench to nibble on while we prepare dinner. Here, I have teamed the tapenade with some eggs, spinach, roasted tomatoes and nuts. My advice is to make a big batch of tapenade and serve it with steak, lamb, chicken and fish. It's also great dolloped over roasted vegetables. Or thin it out with olive oil and lemon juice or apple cider vinegar to make a dressing for your favourite salad.

SOFT-BOILED DUCK EGGS WITH SAUTÉED GREENS AND OLIVE TAPENADE

12 baby truss tomatoes, snipped into 4 portions

3 tablespoons coconut oil or other good-quality fat*

sea salt and freshly ground black pepper

1 bunch of English spinach (about 400 g), trimmed and roughly chopped

3 tablespoons chicken, beef or vegetable stock or water

30 g (¼ cup) goji berries*, soaked in water for 30 minutes, then drained

4 soft-boiled duck eggs (or chicken eggs if you like), peeled

2 tablespoons pine nuts, toasted

4 tablespoons Olive Tapenade (page 247)

* See Glossary

Preheat the oven to 180°C.

Place the tomatoes on a baking tray, drizzle over 1 tablespoon of oil or fat and season with salt and pepper. Roast for 10 minutes until the tomatoes burst and the skins start to blister. Remove from the oven and set aside, keeping warm.

Heat the remaining oil or fat in a large frying pan over medium–high heat. Add the spinach and stock or water and sauté for 2–3 minutes until the spinach is wilted. Season with salt and pepper and stir through the goji berries.

Arrange the sautéed spinach and goji berries on serving plates and sprinkle over the pine nuts. Cut the eggs in half and place on top of the spinach, then sprinkle with some pepper. Add the roasted tomatoes and serve with a ramekin of olive tapenade on the side.

Serves 4

I have always been a fan of curried eggs and this omelette is a fun way to get some healing spices into your diet first thing in the morning. I like to serve this with whatever is in season so be as creative as you like. Another cool thing you can do is make a few extra omelettes to keep in the fridge. Fill them with leftover roasted chicken, pork or lamb and some salad ingredients to create an egg wrap. Or simply slice up an omelette and pop it onto some Indian cauliflower rice (page 212) or add it to your favourite curry for a little egg hit. Always serve with some fermented veg on the side.

CURRIED EGG OMELETTE

2½ tablespoons coconut oil or
  other good-quality fat*
½ red onion, finely chopped
½ red capsicum, finely diced
2 garlic cloves, finely chopped
1 long red chilli, deseeded and
  finely chopped (optional)
sea salt and freshly ground
  black pepper
6 eggs
1½ teaspoons good-quality curry
  powder
1 tablespoon finely chopped
  flat-leaf parsley leaves
1 tablespoon finely chopped
  coriander leaves
16 cherry tomatoes

* See Glossary

Melt 1 tablespoon of oil or fat in a frying pan over medium heat, add the onion and cook for 4–5 minutes until translucent. Add the capsicum and cook for 2 minutes, then stir in the garlic and chilli (if using) and cook for 1 minute until softened. Season with salt and pepper. Remove from the pan and keep warm.

To make the omelette, crack the eggs into a bowl, then add the curry powder, parsley and coriander and beat until combined. Season with salt and pepper.

Heat a non-stick frying pan over medium heat and add 1 teaspoon of oil or fat. Pour in half of the egg mixture and tilt the pan so the mixture covers the base. Spoon half of the cooked onion mixture onto one side of the omelette and cook until the egg is lightly golden underneath and just set on top, 2–3 minutes. Fold the uncovered half of the omelette over the side covered with the cooked onion mixture. Slide onto a serving plate and keep warm. Repeat this process to make a second omelette.

Wipe the pan clean and place over medium–high heat. Melt the remaining oil or fat in the pan, then add the cherry tomatoes and cook, tossing occasionally, for 4 minutes until the tomatoes are heated through and the skins start to blister. Season with a little salt and pepper, if desired. Divide the cherry tomatoes between the plates and serve.

Serves 2 hungry people

As a kid I remember thinking how weird it was that farmers always ate steak and eggs for breakfast. Fast-forward 30-odd years and here I am eating just like the farmers did, though with some extra green veg and nuts. This recipe comes from my dear friend and personal trainer Mike Campbell, a Kiwi who has written a wonderful book called *Alpha Male* and is known for eating 52 different meats over 52 weeks!

PERFECT STEAK AND EGGS WITH KALE AND ALMONDS

Heat a barbecue plate or chargrill pan to hot.

Coat the steaks with 1 tablespoon of oil or fat and season with salt and pepper. Cook the steaks on one side for 2½–3 minutes, or until browned, then flip over and cook for another 2½–3 minutes for medium–rare. Remove from the heat, place the steaks on a plate and cover with foil. Leave to rest for 4–6 minutes.

Meanwhile, heat 1 tablespoon of oil or fat in a large non-stick frying pan over medium heat. Crack the eggs into the pan and cook for 2–3 minutes, or until cooked to your liking. Season the eggs with salt and pepper, then slide onto a plate and keep warm.

Wipe the pan clean with paper towel, then reheat over medium heat with the remaining oil or fat. Add the garlic and cook for 20 seconds until softened and fragrant. Toss in the kale and sauté for 1 minute, then add 3 tablespoons of water and continue to cook for 3–4 minutes, stirring occasionally, until the kale is slightly wilted and cooked through. Add the almonds and season with salt and pepper.

To serve, divide the kale and almonds between serving plates, top with a piece of steak and a fried egg.

Serves 4

4 sirloin steaks (about 120 g each)
3 tablespoons coconut oil or
    other good-quality fat*
sea salt and freshly ground
    black pepper
4 eggs
3 garlic cloves, finely chopped
300 g curly kale (about 1 bunch),
    central stems removed,
    leaves torn
80 g (½ cup) activated almonds,
    toasted and chopped

* See Glossary

Get your kids involved!

HEALTHY KIDS ARE HAPPY KIDS

Sushi rolls
Nut cheese
Nachos
Fritters

KIDS' LUNCHES

Paleo
lunchboxes
rock!

I wasn't a big reader as a kid; however, I did read all of Dr Seuss's books, as I am sure many of you did, too. I still love reading them to my own beautiful girls, and they love them so much they have dressed up as characters from his books at their school's Book Day. In honour of Dr Seuss, I felt it would be great to reinterpret *Green Eggs and Ham*, one of my daughters' favourites, as a perfect school lunch or a picnic recipe that the whole family will enjoy.

GREEN EGGS AND HAM

4 eggs
melted coconut oil, for brushing
4 tablespoons finely chopped mixed herbs (such as flat-leaf parsley, thyme, basil, mint and chervil)
4–6 slices of leg ham, to serve
raw vegetables (lettuce, carrot and celery sticks, cherry tomatoes), to serve

Fill a small saucepan with water and bring to the boil over high heat. Reduce the heat to low so that the water is simmering, then add the eggs and cook for 6–7 minutes. Drain and, when cool enough to handle, peel the eggs under cold running water.

Brush the peeled eggs with a little coconut oil, then roll the eggs in the herbs. Gently press in the herbs with the palm of your hands to create a nice, even coating.

Serve the green eggs with the ham and raw vegetables.

Serves 2

PREP:
20 mins
(+ 5 mins for mayo)
cook:
nil

Sushi rolls are probably my daughters' favourite ever meal — well, aside from paleo nachos, crumbed fish, burgers, bacon and eggs, butter chicken ... Paleo nori rolls are really *really* simple, you just need to replace the usual white rice for cauliflower rice, then you can add the ingredients that you and your family love. A great tip for the cauliflower rice is to fold through some tahini, nut butter or avocado to help bind it a little.

CHICKEN, AVOCADO AND CAULIFLOWER SUSHI

400 g (2 cups) Cauliflower Rice (page 208)
3 tablespoons hulled tahini
sea salt
4 toasted nori sheets*
1 spring onion, julienned
1 cucumber, deseeded and julienned
½ carrot, julienned
½ small daikon*, julienned
½ avocado, sliced into strips
8 small shiso leaves* (optional)
200 g cooked chicken
2 tablespoons Mayonnaise (page 242), plus extra to serve
2 pinches of shichimi togarashi (Japanese chilli spice) (optional)

To serve
white and black sesame seeds, toasted
tamari
wasabi (optional)
sauerkraut (optional)

* See Glossary

Place the cauliflower rice and tahini in a bowl, then season with salt and mix well.

Place a nori sheet on a bamboo sushi mat. Spread one-quarter of the cauliflower rice mix onto half of the nori sheet. Layer the spring onion, cucumber, carrot, daikon, avocado, shiso (if using) and chicken across the middle of the cauliflower rice. Drizzle with some mayonnaise and sprinkle over some shichimi togarashi, if you like.

Starting with the edge closest to you, tightly wrap the roll all the way to the end, then use a little water to seal the ends of the nori together. Trim the ends with a sharp knife, then cut into 2 cm rounds. Repeat with the remaining nori, cauliflower rice and fillings.

Place the sushi pieces on a platter and sprinkle with sesame seeds. Serve with mayonnaise, tamari, wasabi and sauerkraut (if desired).

Serves 4

TIP

If your kids don't like spicy food, simply leave out the shichimi togarashi and wasabi.

We've used purple cauliflower to make the cauliflower rice here, but white cauliflower is fine too! You could also use zucchini or broccoli rice if you'd prefer (page 208).

Kids' snacks in a flash

Celery with nut cheese (page 256) is a great combo. Simply cut celery into 8 cm lengths, then spoon on the nut cheese. You could also sprinkle over some sunflower or pumpkin seeds for extra crunch. Alternatively, serve the nut cheese in a bowl with sticks of celery and other veggies and let the kids dig in.

Eggs are a brilliant snack for kids – and adults for that matter! I make a big batch of hard-boiled eggs and then store them in a container in the fridge for the perfect fast snack. They will last 7 days unpeeled and 5 days peeled.

Cooking is a fantastic activity for kids. It gives them an understanding of where foods comes from, and encourages them to eat healthily. If a child has helped to prepare or cook their own meal or snack, even in some small way, they are much more likely to want to eat it!

To make eggs a bit more fun for kids, slice hard-boiled eggs into halves lengthways. Carefully remove the yolks and place in a bowl. Add a couple of tablespoons of mayonnaise (page 242), then whip the mixture with a wooden spoon until smooth and creamy (you could also use a food processor to do this). Arrange the eggwhites hole-side up, then pipe or spoon the yolk mixture into the holes and sprinkle with some chopped herbs.

Most kids love **guacamole** and it's a great way to get them involved in the kitchen. You'll need to cut the avocados open yourself, but get the kids to scoop out the flesh and mash it with a fork. Stir through some chopped herbs that they like – perhaps coriander or chives. Add a squeeze of lemon juice and a pinch of salt and pepper and you're done. Serve with veggie sticks for dipping, or spread on top of slices of paleo bread (page 257).

Iceberg lettuce and ham salad wraps are great for school lunchboxes. Lay a sheet of baking paper onto a board and place an iceberg leaf on the paper. Spread some mayonnaise (page 242) over the lettuce, then top with ham, grated carrot and beetroot and a little more mayo. Roll up the lettuce, wrap it tightly in the paper and cut in half.

One of the main principles of paleo is the daily inclusion of fermented vegetables and bone broth in your diet because of the amazing benefits they have for gut health. If you have been paleo for a while, your fridge and pantry will be filled with different types of fermented veg and you will have a huge variety to play with at every meal. Here is a great recipe that can be made very quickly if you have some paleo bread and fermented veg on hand. To finish, just add a salad and perhaps some nut cheese (page 256). To take it to another level, add some leftover chicken or smoked fish or cook up some bacon and eggs.

PREP:
10 mins
(+ 10 mins for bread)
COOK:
nil (+ 50 mins for bread)

FRESH VEGGIE AND TZATZIKI SANDWICH

To make the tzatziki, place all the ingredients in a bowl and mix to combine.

To assemble the sandwiches, spread the toasted bread with tzatziki, then top with the rocket, onion, beetroot (if using), radishes, carrot, capsicum and fermented veg. Top with the remaining slices of bread.

Serves 4

8 slices of Seed and Nut Bread (page 256), toasted
1 large handful of baby rocket leaves
½ red onion, thinly sliced
1 beetroot, roasted and thinly sliced (optional)
2 radishes, thinly sliced
1 carrot, julienned
¼ red capsicum, julienned
fermented veggies of your choice

Tzatziki
1 garlic clove, finely chopped
½ Lebanese cucumber, deseeded and grated
150 g coconut yoghurt
1 teaspoon lemon juice, or to taste
1 teaspoon chopped mint leaves
pinch of sumac*

Tips

If your kids are not into onion, simply leave it out. And use any other thinly sliced veggies that you know they will love – cucumber, tomato, anything goes really!

To make this sandwich even faster to prepare, I recommend using a mandoline or julienne peeler to julienne your veggies (see page 13 for more information).

PREP:
15 mins (+ 4 hrs to
soak for cashew cheese)
cook:
25 mins

I cooked this recently with the kids and I am proud to say we now have a new family favourite that is requested on a regular basis! It is grain-, dairy- and legume-free, which ticks all the boxes for me, and is full of top-quality protein, fats and vegetables. And the best news is that it is super bloody delicious. Try adding 50 g of minced liver or heart to the spicy beef recipe for a nutritional boost. I'm sure once you try this, you will be in nacho heaven. Leftovers are awesome to pack for lunch the next day, so triple the recipe for the mince and guacamole. Keep the sweet potato chips separate in the lunchbox so they stay crisp.

PALEO NACHOS

1 large sweet potato, very thinly sliced using a mandoline
3–4 tablespoons coconut oil, melted
sea salt
Cashew Cheese (page 256), to serve (optional)

Spicy Mexican beef
2 tablespoons coconut oil or other good-quality fat*
1 onion, finely chopped
2 garlic cloves, finely chopped
1 long red chilli, deseeded and chopped
500 g beef mince
1 teaspoon smoked paprika
1 teaspoon ground cumin
½ teaspoon ground coriander
1½ tablespoons tomato paste
1 × 400 g can diced tomatoes
freshly ground black pepper

Tomato salsa
2 tomatoes, deseeded and diced
¼ red onion, finely diced
2 tablespoons chopped coriander leaves, plus extra coriander leaves to serve
2 tablespoons lime juice
2 tablespoons extra-virgin olive oil

Guacamole
1 ripe avocado, mashed or diced
1 garlic clove, finely diced
1 tablespoon lime juice
½ teaspoon chilli flakes (optional)
1 tablespoon extra-virgin olive oil

* See Glossary

Preheat the oven to 200°C. Line two large baking trays with baking paper.

Place the sweet potato in a bowl and drizzle over the coconut oil. Toss to coat, then spread the sweet potato onto the trays in a single layer. Bake for 5 minutes, then flip the sweet potato over and return to the oven for about 2 minutes, or until golden and crispy. Season with salt.

To make the spicy Mexican beef, heat the oil or fat in a frying pan over medium–high heat. Add the onion and cook for 5 minutes until translucent. Stir in the garlic and chilli and cook for 1 minute until fragrant. Add the beef and cook, stirring with a wooden spoon to break up any lumps, for 5 minutes until browned. Add the spices and tomato paste and cook for 1 minute, then mix in the tomatoes. Reduce the heat to low and simmer for 10–12 minutes. Season with salt and pepper.

To make the tomato salsa, place all the ingredients in a bowl and mix. Season with salt and pepper.

To make the guacamole, place all the ingredients in a bowl and mix well. Season with salt and pepper.

To assemble the nachos, place the sweet potato chips on a platter or on serving plates, then top with the spicy beef, salsa and guacamole. Garnish with the extra coriander leaves and serve with some cashew cheese, if you like.

Serves 4–6

PREP:
10 mins (+ 2 mins
for pizza sauce &
7 mins for salsa verde)
cook:
13 mins

My goal with all of the meals in this book is to combine an abundance of vegetables with some quality animal protein and cook them in good fats – and these prawn and eggplant pizzas achieve just that. They are also a fun way to serve up some wonderful flavours that will have the family asking for more. Serve with some fermented veg on the side, and enjoy.

EGGPLANT AND PRAWN MINI PIZZAS

1 large eggplant, cut into
    1 cm thick rounds
3 tablespoons coconut oil,
    melted
sea salt and freshly ground
    black pepper
125 ml (½ cup) Pizza Sauce
    (page 185)
2 tablespoons chopped
    flat-leaf parsley
½ red capsicum, roasted,
    peeled and diced
8 cherry tomatoes, sliced
8 yellow teardrop tomatoes,
    sliced
100 g raw king prawns, shelled
    and deveined, chopped
½ teaspoon chilli flakes (optional)
3 tablespoons Salsa Verde
    (page 255)

Preheat the oven to 240°C and line a baking tray with baking paper.

Brush each side of the eggplant with oil, then season with salt and pepper. Place the eggplant slices on the prepared tray and roast in the oven for 5 minutes, or until cooked through and slightly golden. Allow to cool a little before adding the topping.

Spoon 1 tablespoon of pizza sauce over each eggplant slice, then sprinkle on the parsley and top with the capsicum, tomato, prawns and chilli flakes (if using). Season with salt and pepper. Return to the oven and roast for 5–8 minutes, or until the prawns are cooked through and slightly golden.

Drizzle the salsa verde on the pizzas and serve.

Serves 3–4

Tips

Instead of eggplant you could use thickly sliced sweet potato, pumpkin or zucchini. Try scooping some flesh out of the zucchini to make little boats.

You can swap the prawns for prosciutto, ham, salami or even leftover roast chicken (which works a treat with the salsa verde).

I have been lucky enough to spend some time with Michele Chevalley Hedge, who strongly promotes a better future for the coming generations by encouraging parents to cook nutrient-dense foods for their kids. Michele showed me a recipe that she likes to cook for her children and it has become a family favourite in our house as well. We have used chicken but you could substitute turkey, fish, seafood, pork, lamb, beef or pretty much any other animal protein that you love. Always remember to serve these with raw or cooked vegetables and some fermented vegetables.

PREP:
8 mins
COOK:
12 mins

THAI CHICKEN CAKES

Preheat the oven to 180°C and lightly grease an 8-cup muffin tin with coconut oil.

Place the chicken, garlic, spinach, fish sauce, turmeric, coconut cream and ginger in a food processor and pulse a few times until finely chopped.

Spoon the chicken mixture evenly into the prepared tin, then bake for 12 minutes, or until cooked through. Cool slightly for 5 minutes before turning out. The chicken cakes will release a little bit of liquid when cooked, so drain off the liquid before you remove them from the tin.

Arrange the lettuce cups on a large platter or serving plates. Place two chicken cakes inside each cup, along with some avocado, cucumber and coriander, and squeeze over some lime juice.

Serves 4

500 g chicken thigh fillets,
cut into pieces
2 garlic cloves, chopped
1 large handful of baby
spinach leaves
2 teaspoons fish sauce
½ teaspoon ground turmeric
3 tablespoons coconut cream
1 teaspoon finely grated ginger

To serve
4 iceberg lettuce leaves, trimmed
into cups
1 avocado, sliced
½ Lebanese cucumber, sliced
1 small handful of coriander
leaves
1 lime, halved

TIP

Make a big batch of these chicken cakes, as they freeze really well. Simply pull a few out of the freezer in the morning and pop into your kids' lunchboxes – they should be defrosted and ready to eat by lunchtime. Store in the freezer for up to 3 months.

Spreads & dips in a flash

Nut butters are a great way to increase your protein and good fat intake. To make almond butter, pop a few cups of activated almonds in a food processor and process for 5 minutes until smooth. Add a drizzle of coconut, macadamia or olive oil if it's too thick, and process until you reach your desired consistency. I like to get experimental with nut butters – mix it up by adding different kinds of nuts, such as Brazil nuts, macadamia nuts, cashews and pistachios.

You can also try making **delicious seed butters**, following the same process as for nut butter. I love making a bright green spread by blending up activated pumpkin seeds until smooth and thick (adding a drizzle of coconut, macadamia or olive oil if necessary to loosen things up). Season with a touch of salt if needed and serve on toasted paleo bread (page 257).

Add tahini (a paste made from sesame seeds) to your nut butter for extra creaminess and nutrients. You could also try adding some ground spices, such as turmeric and cumin, for extra flavour and colour.

Avocado makes the greatest instant dip – roughly mash it then stir through some extra-virgin olive oil, crushed garlic, finely chopped chilli and salt and pepper. If you have a little more time, roast some beets, carrots or pumpkin until soft, then mash and mix as above. Serve these dips with fresh veggie sticks.

Dairy-free pesto is so easy to make and is fabulous served as a dip. Pack your food processor with basil leaves, then add a couple of chopped garlic cloves, some toasted pine nuts, lemon juice and salt and pepper. Process until combined, then add enough extra-virgin olive oil or macadamia oil to form a thick paste. You could also use parsley leaves, coriander leaves or even rocket instead of the basil leaves.

Nut cheese (page 256) is a delicious spread to have on hand and so simple to make. Macadamia nuts and cashews are most commonly used, as they develop a really creamy texture after soaking and processing. I like to blend some ground turmeric through the cheese as it's such a powerful medicinal spice and has a gorgeous flavour. Tahini, garlic powder and freshly cracked pepper also make a delicious flavour combination to add to nut cheese.

This is my favourite recipe to teach up on stage. I get people out of the audience to taste it and I always ask for people who hate liver. I try to get at least one kid up on stage, too. I crumb a chicken liver and a chicken breast and cook them both until they are golden (making sure the liver is still pink in the middle). Then I ask my volunteers to try the liver first — nine times out of ten they love it. Then they'll try the breast and nine times out of ten they say that it is boring and they would rather the liver. So give this recipe a try — you and your kids might just love it too!

CHICKEN LIVER NUGGETS

12 chicken livers, sinew removed
2 eggs
3 tablespoons coconut milk or
    almond milk
200 g (2 cups) almond meal or
    macadamia meal
½ teaspoon garlic powder
½ teaspoon onion powder
1 teaspoon dried parsley
1 teaspoon dried mint
1 teaspoon sea salt
½ teaspoon freshly ground black
    pepper
125 g (1 cup) tapioca flour*
250 ml (1 cup) coconut oil or
    other good-quality fat*
lemon wedges, to serve

Herb aioli
100 g (⅓ cup) Aioli (page 242)
½ teaspoon finely chopped
    flat-leaf parsley leaves
½ teaspoon finely snipped chives
½ teaspoon finely grated
    lemon zest

See Glossary

To make the herb aioli, mix all the ingredients in a bowl and set aside until needed.

Place the livers on paper towel and pat dry.

Crack the eggs into a bowl and whisk with the coconut or almond milk until well combined. In another bowl, combine the almond or macadamia meal, garlic and onion powders, parsley, mint, salt and pepper and mix well. Place the tapioca flour in a third bowl.

Working with one piece at a time, coat the chicken livers in the tapioca flour, shaking off any excess, then dip each liver in the egg mixture and roll in the nut crumb mixture to evenly coat. (If there are any uncoated areas, simply dab on a little more egg mixture and re-coat with the nut crumb.)

Heat the oil or fat in a large deep frying pan over medium heat. Test the heat of the oil or fat by placing a small piece of chicken liver in the pan. When the fat or oil sizzles around the chicken, it has reached its ideal heat. Add the chicken liver nuggets, in batches, and cook for 1½–2 minutes on each side, or until golden brown and cooked through. Remove the nuggets from the pan using tongs or a slotted spoon and drain on paper towel. Season with salt and pepper, if desired. Allow the nuggets to cool a little before serving with the herb aioli and lemon wedges.

Serves 4

My dear friend Michelle Tam is the world-famous blogger who created Nom Nom Paleo. A couple of years ago I was lucky enough to work with Michelle and her husband Henry Fong in their home in San Francisco, filming and recreating some of their favourite family recipes. One of them was their famous egg foo young: a simple dish that can easily be made for breakfast, school or work lunches or dinner. My advice is to make as many as possible so you have leftovers to keep in the fridge to eat for a snack or to take on picnics. Thanks Michelle and Henry. You guys rock.

NOM NOM'S EGG FOO YOUNG-ISH

5 eggs
1 teaspoon snipped chives
sea salt
30 g (3½ tablespoons) coconut flour
½ teaspoon baking soda
100 g frozen spinach, thawed and squeezed dry (you should end up with about 50 g)
100 g (⅔ cup) ham (or any leftover meat), finely diced
½ teaspoon apple cider vinegar
coconut oil, for frying
sugar-free chilli sauce or Guacamole (page 52), to serve (optional)

In a large bowl, whisk together the eggs and chives and season with some salt. Sift in the coconut flour and baking soda. Add the spinach, ham and vinegar and stir to make a thick batter.

Heat 1 tablespoon of coconut oil in a large non-stick frying pan over medium heat. Scoop ¼ cup of batter into the pan and flatten to form a fritter. Cook the fritters, in batches, for 2 minutes, then flip over and cook for a further minute or so until cooked through. Repeat with the remaining batter.

Serve the fritters topped with some chilli sauce or guacamole, if desired, but they are wonderful eaten just as they are.

Serves 2

Let's talk about the white elephant in the room … bread! Many people are reluctant to adopt a paleo-inspired lifestyle because they are terrified of giving up bread. So instead of depriving your loved ones of one of life's luxuries, why not make paleo bread? Once you have a paleo bread recipe, you can recreate your favourite dishes. This recipe is as simple as it gets: a chicken sandwich made with fresh and delicious ingredients. You can toast the bread for extra texture if you like or, for something new, convert the sandwich into a delicious chicken salad by crisping up the bread and turning it into croutons.

PREP:
10 mins
(+ 5 mins for mayo
& 10 mins for bread)
COOK:
(+1 hr 20 mins
for bread)

CHICKEN AND CELERIAC SANDWICHES WITH AVOCADO AND SAUERKRAUT

Place the chicken, celeriac, mayo, lemon zest and juice, chervil and tarragon in a bowl and mix well. Season with salt and pepper.

To assemble, place four slices of bread on a work surface or chopping board. Top the bread with some radicchio, then add the chicken filling, avocado and sauerkraut. Sprinkle some dill on each sandwich and place another slice of bread on top.

Serves 4

1 cooked chicken breast or 2 chicken thigh fillets, chopped into small pieces
⅛ celeriac (about 120 g), julienned
4 tablespoons Mayonnaise (page 242)
1 teaspoon finely grated lemon zest
1 teaspoon lemon juice
1 tablespoon chopped chervil sprigs
1 teaspoon chopped tarragon leaves
sea salt and freshly ground black pepper
8 slices of Nic's Paleo Bread (page 257)
½ radicchio, trimmed and roughly chopped
1 avocado, sliced
4 tablespoons sauerkraut
2 dill fronds

EAT
A SALAD
EVERY DAY

Add nuts and seeds for extra crunch!

**Beetroot
Leeks
Salmon
Pomegranates
Rocket**

SALADS

**SLICE,
DRESS, TOSS,
SERVE!**

This recipe really sums up the celebration that paleo eating is for me: an abundance of vibrant vegetables served with a homemade dressing and a handful of seeds and fresh herbs. It's great served with a grilled, steamed or poached piece of meat or some fried eggs, along with a few spoons of fermented vegetables. You can change the dressing to make this slaw match any cuisine: use tahini for a Middle Eastern dish; chimichurri (page 251) to make it South American; nam jim (page 253) for a South East Asian feel; or to create a classic coleslaw, simply use some homemade mayonnaise and dill.

ASIAN SLAW

225 g (3 cups) shredded Chinese cabbage (wong bok)

225 g (3 cups) shredded red cabbage

1 large carrot, julienned

5 large radishes, julienned

4 spring onions, white and green part, finely sliced

1–2 long red chillies, deseeded and julienned

1 red capsicum, julienned

1–2 large handfuls of coriander leaves

100 g bean sprouts

2 tablespoons sesame seeds, toasted, plus extra to serve

sea salt and freshly ground black pepper

Asian dressing

3 tablespoons miso paste or tahini

1 tablespoon tamari or coconut aminos*

2 teaspoons finely grated ginger

1 garlic clove, finely chopped

2 tablespoons apple cider vinegar

1 tablespoon Mayonnaise (page 242)

1 tablespoon lemon juice or yuzu* juice

1 teaspoon honey (optional)

3 tablespoons avocado oil or olive oil

2 tablespoons sesame oil

See Glossary

To make the dressing, in a small bowl, whisk together the miso or tahini, tamari or coconut aminos, ginger, garlic, vinegar, mayonnaise, lemon or yuzu juice and honey (if using). Slowly whisk in the avocado or olive oil and sesame oil until emulsified. Set aside.

To make the slaw, combine all the ingredients in a large bowl, add half of the dressing and toss gently. Add a little more dressing if required, then store any remaining dressing in a sealed glass jar in the fridge (use within 3–4 days).

Check the seasoning and add more salt and pepper if needed. To finish, sprinkle on some extra toasted sesame seeds.

Serves 6 as a side

Tip

To make this dish even faster to prepare, I recommend using a mandoline or julienne peeler to julienne your veggies (see page 13 for more information).

PREP:
10 mins (+ 5 mins
for macadamia cheese &
5 mins for green
goddess dressing)
COOK:
nil

I am a sucker for asparagus when it's in season and I love to use it in as many different ways as possible: grilled alongside some eggs and bacon for breakfast, or added to a spring vegetable and chicken soup for lunch, or incorporated into a stunning stir-fry of beef, broccoli and asparagus for dinner. If you are looking for a way to wow your guests, then look no further. Team this salad with grilled fish for a truly memorable dinner.

SHAVED ASPARAGUS SALAD WITH GREEN GODDESS DRESSING

3 bunches of asparagus (about 350 g), woody ends trimmed
250 g heirloom cherry tomatoes, cut into quarters
1 Lebanese cucumber, deseeded and finely diced

Herb dressing
1 tablespoon finely snipped chives
1 tablespoon finely chopped flat-leaf parsley
3 tablespoons lemon juice or apple cider vinegar
4 tablespoons extra-virgin olive oil
sea salt and freshly ground black pepper

To serve
4 tablespoons Green Goddess Dressing (page 250)
100 g Macadamia Cheese (page 256)
baby basil leaves

Using a vegetable peeler or mandoline, shave the asparagus into thin ribbons starting from the bottom end. Place the asparagus ribbons in one bowl, and the tomato and cucumber in another bowl.

To make the herb dressing, combine the chives, parsley, lemon juice or vinegar and olive oil in a bowl and whisk to combine. Season with salt and pepper.

Pour half of the dressing over the asparagus and the remainder over the tomato and cucumber. Gently toss until evenly coated.

Arrange the asparagus on serving plates, then top with the tomato and cucumber. Smear a tablespoon of green goddess dressing on each plate, then sprinkle with the macadamia cheese. Drizzle over some extra herb dressing and finish with some basil leaves on top.

Serves 4 as a side

This recipe takes me back to my early days working as a chef in commercial kitchens. There were versions of this salad in so many restaurants. Some would have Parmigiano Reggiano shaved over the top, some would add roast chicken and some would crumble on crispy bacon. And the dressings would be different, too: from a Spanish sherry vinaigrette or a lemon and mustard dressing all the way through to a creamy mayonnaise-based version. Here I have kept it traditional by using a simple balsamic dressing. Have a play around as it works well with shaved fennel or mushrooms instead of the pear, or swap out the rocket for radicchio or cabbage.

PREP:
8 mins
COOK:
nil

ROCKET AND PEAR SALAD WITH BALSAMIC DRESSING

To make the dressing, mix all of the ingredients in a small bowl.

In a large bowl, combine the rocket, pear, walnuts and half of the dressing and gently toss.

Transfer the salad to a large serving dish and drizzle over more dressing, if desired.

Serves 4 as a side

150 g baby rocket leaves
2 beurre bosc pears, cored and thinly sliced
80 g (heaped ¾ cup) activated walnuts, toasted

Balsamic dressing
2 teaspoons Dijon mustard
3 tablespoons balsamic vinegar or coconut aminos*
125 ml (½ cup) extra-virgin olive oil
pinch each of sea salt and freshly ground black pepper

* See Glossary

'Less is more' has always been and will always be a chef's mantra. This entails letting the ingredients shine as much as possible. Sure there are amazing recipes – such as curries – that include 20 ingredients but the underlying factor to these complex dishes is that everything is in balance without one flavour dominating another. And then we have dishes like this one which is really just some awesome crunchy pristine leaves lightly coated with a playful dressing that brings everything to life. I encourage you to play around with different dressings and vinaigrettes and become the master salad maker at home.

FRESH COS SALAD WITH MUSTARD VINAIGRETTE

4 baby cos lettuces, leaves
separated
2 handfuls of mixed herbs
(such as tarragon, dill, mint,
flat-leaf parsley and basil
leaves)
80 ml (⅓ cup) Mustard Vinaigrette
(page 252)
sea salt and freshly ground
black pepper

Tear the cos leaves into smaller pieces.

Combine the herbs and cos in a serving bowl. Drizzle on the mustard dressing and serve immediately. Add a little salt and pepper, if you like.

Serves 4

This dish includes two under-utilised ingredients that I believe should be more prominent in our seasonal cooking. And what better way to use them than in a salad? The fennel, with its delicious sweet aniseed flavour, works so well with seafood, chicken, pork or lamb and the celeriac adds a robust and satisfying earthiness. This salad becomes the star of the table when paired perfectly with a grilled piece of fish or some roast pork with crackling or a chicken schnitzel.

FENNEL AND CELERIAC SALAD WITH WALNUT AND MUSTARD DRESSING

½ celeriac (about 350 g), peeled
juice of ½ lemon
1 large fennel bulb
4 brussels sprouts
80 g good-quality sauerkraut (optional)
1 tablespoon finely snipped chives

Walnut and mustard dressing
4 tablespoons apple cider vinegar
1½ teaspoons wholegrain mustard
3 tablespoons macadamia oil or extra-virgin olive oil
3 tablespoons walnut oil
50 g (½ cup) activated walnuts, toasted and chopped
sea salt and freshly ground black pepper

Finely slice the celeriac using a mandoline or sharp knife, then cut into thin matchstick-like strips. Alternatively, you could use a julienne peeler to cut the celeriac into thin strips. Place in a bowl of cold water and add the lemon juice to prevent the celeriac from oxidising.

Next, finely shave the fennel using a mandoline or sharp knife and add to the celeriac in the lemon water. Finely slice the brussels sprouts and set aside until needed.

To make the dressing, combine the vinegar, mustard and oils in a bowl and whisk well. Stir in the walnuts and season with salt and pepper.

Drain the fennel and celeriac and place in a bowl along with the brussels sprouts, sauerkraut (if using) and chives. Pour in just enough dressing to coat and season with more salt and pepper, if needed. Toss gently and transfer to a large platter, spooning some more dressing over the top.

Serves 4 as a side

When does a salad become a meal in itself? When it is nutritionally balanced with good sources of fat and protein and it leaves you feeling satiated. And that is exactly what this salad does. We always have soft- or hard-boiled eggs in the fridge for salads just like this one. Here I have used raw broccolini but feel free to lightly steam it if you prefer. You could also add some dried blueberries or currants if you are looking for a sweet boost. Leftover roast chicken, lamb, pork, beef or seafood would make perfect additions too.

PREP:
20 mins
COOK:
nil

RAW BEETROOT SALAD

To make the dressing, combine all of the ingredients in a bowl and whisk well.

To make the salad, place all the ingredients in a large bowl. Add the dressing and gently toss until everything is evenly coated. Season with salt and pepper.

Arrange the salad on a platter, then top with the eggs. Season with more salt or pepper, if desired, and sprinkle on sesame seeds (if using) to finish.

Serves 3–4 as a main

1 large beetroot, grated
½ bunch of frisee, leaves
separated
1 bunch of broccolini, woody
ends trimmed, thinly sliced
4 stalks of kale, stalks discarded
and leaves torn
3 tablespoons roughly chopped
activated walnuts
1 large handful of mixed fresh
herbs (such as mint, flat-leaf
parsley, dill and chervil)
seeds of ½ pomegranate
3 tablespoons goji berries*
(optional)

Tahini dressing
3 tablespoons hulled tahini
2 tablespoons apple cider
vinegar or lemon juice
2 tablespoons extra-virgin
olive oil
pinch each of sumac* and
ground cumin
sea salt and freshly ground
black pepper

To serve
4 soft-boiled eggs, peeled
and halved
sesame seeds, toasted (optional)

* See Glossary

Recently I filmed an episode of *Moveable Feast* (a TV series I host in the USA) in an avocado grove in the hills of California with the 'too hot tamales', chefs Mary Sue Milliken and Susan Feniger. Two of the coolest people in southern California, these living food legends taught me so much about Mexican cuisine in the small amount of time I had with them. The stand-out for me was crispy fried avocado, which they used in a dish. I thought it was so good it should be renamed and served by itself.

AVOCADO FRIES

50 g (⅓ cup) tapioca flour*
150 g (1 cup) white and black
   sesame seeds
2 avocados, cut into 2 cm thick
   slices
3–4 tablespoons coconut oil
½ teaspoon ground spice (such
   as curry powder, smoked
   paprika, cumin or turmeric)
   (optional)
sea salt
lemon wedges, to serve

* See Glossary

Whisk the tapioca and 80 ml of water in a bowl until combined. Place the sesame seeds in a small, shallow bowl.

Dip the avocado slices into the tapioca mixture to coat, then coat with the sesame seeds, patting down gently.

Heat the coconut oil to 160°C in a frying pan or saucepan. To test the temperature, drop a small piece of avocado in the oil – it should bubble instantly around the edges.

Working in batches, fry the avocado for 50–60 seconds on each side or until the sesame seeds are golden. Drain on paper towel and season with a little spice (if using) and salt.

Arrange on a platter and serve with some lemon wedges to squeeze over the top.

Serves 4 as a snack

PREP:
15 mins
COOK:
nil

I adore salads like this that use top-quality spices, herbs, fruit and vegetables, are put together in a matter of minutes and just blow your tastebuds away. My advice is to make a few delicious salad dressings and sauces throughout the week and keep them in the fridge to use in your salads, with cooked meat, seafood or vegetables, or to stir into your favourite soups. Play around with ingredients that are in season and add a spoonful or two of fermented vegetables for gut health.

GYPSY SALAD

250 g cherry tomatoes, halved
1 Lebanese cucumber, halved
  lengthways and thinly sliced
½ red onion, finely sliced
5 medjool dates, stoned
  and sliced
½ yellow capsicum, deseeded
  and finely sliced
1 red capsicum, finely sliced
½ green capsicum, finely sliced
1 large handful of mint leaves
  (about 15 g)
1 large handful of flat-leaf parsley
  leaves (about 15 g)
juice of ½ lemon
3 tablespoons extra-virgin
  olive oil

Coconut dressing
1 garlic clove, finely chopped
1 small red chilli, deseeded and
  finely chopped
½ teaspoon ground cumin
½ teaspoon sumac*, plus extra
  to serve
100 g coconut yoghurt
juice of ½ lemon
sea salt and freshly ground
  black pepper

See Glossary

To make the coconut dressing, combine the garlic, chilli, cumin, sumac, coconut yoghurt and lemon juice in a bowl, season with a little salt and pepper and mix well.

To make the salad, place all the ingredients in a large bowl, season with salt and pepper and gently toss to combine.

Place the salad on a serving dish and drizzle the coconut dressing on top.

Sprinkle with some extra sumac to finish.

Serves 4 as a side

Salad dressings & toppings in a flash

To make a **zingy Italian dressing**, combine some extra-virgin olive oil, apple cider vinegar, finely chopped garlic and red capsicum, Dijon mustard, dried oregano and marjoram, salt and pepper in a jar with a screw-top lid. Close tightly and shake until the dressing thickens.

For something a little different, try an **orange and walnut dressing**. Simply whisk some orange juice with apple cider vinegar, olive oil and crushed walnuts and season with a touch of salt and pepper.

Adding seeds and nuts to your salad gives fabulous texture and flavour, as well as providing extra nutrition. Toast up a big batch of sunflower seeds, pumpkin seeds, flaxseeds and sesame seeds, then store in an airtight container ready to sprinkle over salads.

One of the keys to making a killer salad is to make sure you wash and dry your salad leaves properly. If your leaves are wet the dressing won't be absorbed properly and your salad will be soggy.
I always use a salad spinner to dry my leaves – they are inexpensive and save so much time.

To make a simple **dukkah**, separately toast some pine nuts, sesame seeds, coriander seeds and cumin seeds until golden and fragrant. Cool, then crush using a mortar and pestle or food processor. Transfer to a bowl and stir through a pinch of chilli powder and some salt and pepper. Dukkah is lovely sprinkled over most salads, but it's particularly delicious with roasted pumpkin or egg salads.

HERBS add so much more flavour to salads and it's almost impossible to overdo it! For salads I generally avoid the tougher varieties like rosemary and sage, and opt for parsley, mint, dill, tarragon, coriander, chervil and lemon balm. You can mix and match these herbs to suit your own taste.

Be careful not to overdress your salad - use just enough to coat the ingredients. If you add too much it will become wet and soggy. Also, be super gentle when tossing to avoid bruising the leaves.

My dear friend Manu Feildel is a classically trained French chef from Brittany on the French coast. French cuisine is one of my favourites and I asked him if he would share a salad that fits the paleo philosophy. He told me about his leek salad with eggs, bacon and tomato, which sounded bloody good to me. When we were shooting this recipe we found the most gorgeous baby leeks but if you can't find any, simply use larger leeks and cook them for a little longer, or for a variation replace the leeks with grilled asparagus or zucchini. Thanks Manu and *bon appetit*!

PREP:
10 mins (+ 5 mins for vinaigrette)
COOK:
2 mins (+ 13 mins for vinaigrette)

MANU'S BABY LEEKS WITH SOFT-BOILED EGG AND TRUFFLED BACON AND SHERRY VINAIGRETTE

Bring a saucepan of lightly salted water to the boil. Add the leeks and cook until tender, about 1 minute. Drain and refresh in ice-cold water. Drain again, shaking off any excess water, and pat dry with paper towel.

Place the chives, tomato and olive oil in a bowl, season with salt and pepper and toss gently to combine. Set aside until needed.

Mix the bacon and sherry vinaigrette with the truffle oil.

To serve, arrange the leeks on a serving platter or on two serving plates, scatter on the tomato and chive mixture, then slice the egg in half and pop on top. Drizzle over the truffled bacon and sherry vinaigrette to finish.

Serves 2 as a starter

15 baby leeks, trimmed and washed
2 tablespoons finely snipped chives
2 Roma tomatoes, peeled, deseeded and finely diced
1 tablespoon extra-virgin olive oil
sea salt and freshly ground black pepper
4 tablespoons Bacon and Sherry Vinaigrette (page 250)
1 tablespoon truffle oil (see note)
1 soft-boiled egg, peeled

Note
Truffle oil is an oil that has been infused with truffle, a fungus that grows underground. It has a strong, mushroom-like flavour and is available from gourmet food stores.

Salmon roe was one of the first foods my daughters Chilli and Indii ate when they started on solids. To this day it is their favourite food in the world. I think it is because the slightly salty and sweet flavour combines so well with the delicious oil and fattiness, and let's not forget the texture and the pleasurable popping sensation when you drop the roe in your mouth. Recently the girls have started embracing sashimi, which I am really excited about, as I know how wonderful sustainably sourced raw fish is for our health. Here is a simple preparation that teams the roe and fish with some cress and fennel and a delicious dressing.

SALMON, FENNEL AND WATERCRESS SALAD

2 baby fennel bulbs, finely sliced
1 large handful of watercress
　leaves
1 handful of dill fronds
1 handful of micro herbs
　(optional)
1 tablespoon chervil sprigs
500 g smoked salmon
6 caper berries*, halved
2 tablespoons salmon roe
sea salt and freshly ground
　black pepper

Mustard and honey dressing
juice of 1 lemon
1 tablespoon wholegrain mustard
1 tablespoon honey
4 tablespoons extra-virgin
　olive oil

* See Glossary

To make the mustard and honey dressing, place the lemon juice, mustard and honey in a small bowl. Slowly whisk in the olive oil until emulsified. Season with salt and pepper.

To make the salad, place the fennel, watercress, dill, micro herbs (if using) and chervil in a bowl. Drizzle on a small amount of dressing to lightly coat the herbs. (Be careful not to add too much dressing as the herbs are very delicate.)

Arrange the smoked salmon on a large platter. Gently scatter the dressed salad over the salmon, then add the caper berries and salmon roe. Drizzle on the remaining dressing, if desired, and season with a little salt and pepper.

Serves 4 as a starter

Nothing says summer more to me than a delicious raw fish and vegetable salad. This can be eaten for breakfast, lunch or dinner and takes no time at all to put together. All you need is a mandoline or julienne peeler to help speed up chopping the vegetables, then slice the fish and make the most delicious salad dressing on the planet (which I love because the fish sauce is fermented). If you don't fancy raw fish, simply add some cooked prawns or chicken, beef, lamb or pork. Or if you really want to blow your tastebuds away, try some roasted duck.

ASIAN CEVICHE SALAD

30 g (scant ½ cup) finely
  shredded white cabbage
30 g (scant ½ cup) finely
  shredded red cabbage
1 carrot, julienned
1 red Asian shallot, finely sliced
1 handful of bean sprouts
1 handful of mint leaves
1 handful of coriander leaves
1 handful of Thai basil leaves
200 g snapper fillets, skinned and
  finely sliced on the diagonal
sea salt
3 tablespoons chopped activated
  cashews

Coriander dressing
2 tablespoons very finely
  chopped coriander leaves
4 tablespoons lime juice
1 teaspoon finely grated ginger
1 garlic clove, finely chopped
1 small green chilli, deseeded
  and finely chopped
1 teaspoon fish sauce
1½ teaspoons coconut sugar*
  or honey
1 tablespoon macadamia oil or
  olive oil

* See Glossary

To make the coriander dressing, combine all of the ingredients in a small bowl and stir well.

Combine the cabbages, carrot, shallot, bean sprouts and herbs in a bowl and gently toss.

Pour half of the dressing over the cabbage salad. Add the fish, season to taste and gently mix to combine. Arrange the salad in serving bowls, pour more dressing over the top and sprinkle with the cashews.

Serves 2 as a main

TIPS

You'll need a very sharp knife to finely slice the raw fish for this recipe.

If you can't find any snapper, you can also use tuna or mackerel.

This recipe is one of those dishes that looks a lot harder than it actually is and is extremely satisfying to prepare. For me, seared or raw sashimi-grade fish – such as wild sustainable tuna, salmon or kingfish – teamed with a simple salad and an intoxicating dressing is just a starting point. From here you can add avocado, soft-boiled egg, toasted nori, kelp noodles, togarashi (a Japanese chilli and sesame seed seasoning) or perhaps some fermented daikon or a dollop of Asian-flavoured mayonnaise.

PREP:
15 mins
(+ 15 mins to stand)
COOK:
2 mins

JAPANESE TUNA SALAD

To make the dressing, combine the tamari or coconut aminos, vinegar, lemon juice, coconut sugar or honey and bonito flakes in a bowl. Mix well and set aside.

Meanwhile, place the wakame in a bowl filled with cold water and soak for 15 minutes, or until the wakame has expanded. Drain off the water and place on paper towel to soak up any excess moisture.

Strain the dressing through a sieve and press all the liquid through. Discard the bonito flakes. Add the mustard powder, onion, macadamia oil and sesame oil and mix until well combined.

Rub the tuna with the coconut oil and season with salt and pepper. Heat a barbecue plate or chargrill pan to hot and cook the tuna for 30 seconds on each side, or until lightly golden. Remove from the heat and set aside.

Mix the wakame, cucumber, salad leaves and spring onion in a large bowl and gently toss through half of the dressing. Add a little sea salt if needed.

Arrange the salad on serving plates or a large platter. Using a very sharp knife, slice the tuna into 5 mm thick slices and place on top of the salad. Spoon the remaining dressing over the tuna and salad, then sprinkle with the nori and serve.

Serves 4

2 tablespoons dried wakame*
500 g sashimi-grade tuna, cut into 4 long fillets
1 tablespoon coconut oil, melted
sea salt and freshly ground black pepper
1 Lebanese cucumber, finely sliced lengthways using a mandoline, then cut in half lengthways (discard the seeds)
2 large handfuls of mizuna leaves (see note)
1 handful of baby shiso leaves*
2 spring onions, julienned
1 nori sheet*, cut into thin strips 5 cm long

Bonito dressing
3 tablespoons tamari or coconut aminos*
2½ tablespoons apple cider vinegar
1 teaspoon lemon juice
½ teaspoon coconut sugar* or honey
2 tablespoons bonito flakes*
½ tablespoon mustard powder
½ onion, finely chopped
1 tablespoon macadamia oil
3 teaspoons sesame oil

* See Glossary

Note

Mizuna is a herb with a peppery flavour that is commonly used in Japanese cuisine. It is available from Asian grocers. If you can't find mizuna, use baby rocket leaves instead.

PREP:
5 mins
(+ 5 mins for aioli)
COOK:
3 mins

Could there be a greater combination than that of succulent freshly cooked prawns served over a bucket of ice with a little spicy mayonnaise? Buy the best wild caught and sustainable raw prawns you can find, either fresh or frozen (these days techniques are so advanced that the prawns are snap-frozen on the boats!). I often slightly undercook my prawns as I think it makes them sweeter and more delicious. Make sure you keep the heads and shells to make prawn stock. As for the sauce, play around with different spices, herbs and flavours such as horseradish, wasabi, chilli and mustard. Never stop experimenting.

PERFECT PRAWN SALAD

16 raw king prawns
watercress sprigs, to serve

Harissa and preserved lemon aioli
1½–2 teaspoons harissa paste, or to taste
250 g (1 cup) Aioli (page 242)
1 teaspoon finely chopped preserved lemon zest

Cook the prawns in salted boiling water for 2–3 minutes, or until pink and firm. Transfer the prawns to a bowl of ice-cold water and leave for 3–5 minutes, or until the prawns are completely cold.

Meanwhile, make the harissa and preserved lemon aioli. Combine all of the ingredients in a small bowl and mix until smooth. Add more aioli if the flavour is too spicy for your liking, or add more harissa if you prefer it extra spicy.

Serve the prawns in a bucket with ice, with the aioli and watercress on the side. Set out a bowl for people to discard the shells.

Serves 4 as a starter

When summer hits and the weather is warm, we always look for quick ways to get meals on the table. As you probably know by now, I love to cook outdoors and I feel that this recipe sums up my cooking style: quick, simple and utterly delicious. Squid is the ultimate fast food – it needs only a few minutes on the grill to sear, become tender, get a little colour and take on a smoky flavour. Be careful: if you overcook it, it will become quite tough. (Interestingly, if you choose to cook it for a long time over a low temperature it will soften.) This dish is about combining ingredients that work well together: squid, capers, fennel, lemon and fresh mint and parsley. Now you are cooking like a pro.

SQUID SALAD WITH FENNEL AND BURNT LEMON

600 g cleaned baby squid tubes (including tentacles), halved lengthways and scored on the inside (ask your fishmonger to do this)
1 tablespoon coconut oil, melted

Salad
1 large fennel bulb, finely sliced
2 long red chillies, deseeded and finely chopped
2 red Asian shallots, finely sliced
3 tablespoons salted baby capers, rinsed and patted dry
1 handful of mint leaves
1 handful of flat-leaf parsley leaves
2 lemons, halved
80 ml (⅓ cup) lemon-infused extra-virgin olive oil
sea salt and freshly ground black pepper

Preheat a barbecue plate or chargrill pan to medium–high.

To make the salad, toss the fennel, chilli, shallot, capers and herbs in a bowl. Cook the lemon halves cut-side down on the barbecue for 3–5 minutes until charred. Remove and squeeze the juice from two of the lemon halves over the salad (reserve the remaining halves to serve). Add the lemon-infused olive oil and some salt and pepper and toss gently.

Season the squid with salt and pepper. Add the coconut oil to the barbecue plate or pan and cook the squid for 1 minute on each side, or until cooked through and lightly charred. Toss with the salad and serve immediately with the reserved charred lemon halves.

Serves 2 as a main

Middle Eastern flavours rock! I have been a huge fan ever since I started using their spice combinations and their abundant fresh herbs in my cooking. Fattoush is a classic Middle Eastern salad of seasonal vegetables and herbs, seasoned with sumac, dressed with lemon juice and olive oil and tossed together with some toasted flatbread. I have replaced the traditional bread with a grain-free option to give the wonderful texture that we love in this dish. I have also added some grilled prawns (or you could use chicken) for extra protein and flavour.

PREP:
15 mins (+ 5 mins for pita breads)
COOK:
15 mins (+ 15 mins for pita breads)

FATTOUSH WITH PRAWNS

Preheat the oven to 170°C and line a large baking tray with baking paper.

Season the prawns with salt and pepper. Melt the coconut oil in a large frying pan over medium–high heat. Cook the prawns in batches of 4–5 for 1 minute on each side. Set aside.

Place the pita breads on the lined baking tray. Brush with a little olive oil and sprinkle with 1 teaspoon of sumac. Bake for 5–10 minutes, or until golden and crisp. When cool enough to handle, break into bite-sized pieces.

In a large bowl, whisk the lemon juice, garlic and a pinch of salt and pepper with ¼ teaspoon of sumac and the remaining olive oil. Add the tomato, cucumber, onion, radish, capsicum, mixed herbs and pita pieces and mix well with your hands. Toss in the prawns and the pan juices. Transfer to a serving platter and sprinkle on the remaining sumac to finish.

Serves 4 as a main

16 raw king prawns, shelled and deveined, tails left intact
sea salt and freshly ground black pepper
1 tablespoon coconut oil
2 Coconut Pita Breads (page 257) or other paleo pita breads (see note)
4 tablespoons extra-virgin olive oil
1 tablespoon sumac*
3 tablespoons lemon juice
2 garlic cloves, finely chopped
4 tomatoes, diced
1 Lebanese cucumber, deseeded and sliced
1 red onion, sliced
4 radishes, finely sliced
1 red capsicum, cut into 2 cm pieces
2 large handfuls of mixed herbs (such as coriander, mint, dill and flat-leaf parsley)

See Glossary

Note

Paleo pita breads are usually made from coconut flour rather than a grain-based flour. They are available from health food stores.

When I'm travelling around the world and eating a lot of different dishes, the ones that really resonate always feature perfectly balanced flavours and pristine ingredients. Ceviche is one such dish, where fresh, seasonal ingredients are combined with the most delicious and simple-to-make dressing. I recommend making this when the weather warms up – just pop the ceviche and witlof on the table and let everyone help themselves.

CEVICHE WITH POMEGRANATE AND MANGO

500 g fish fillets (such as snapper, tuna or mackerel) cut into 8 mm cubes
½ teaspoon sea salt
juice of 5 limes
4 tablespoons extra-virgin olive oil
2 tablespoons apple cider vinegar
½ red onion, finely chopped
1 long red chilli, deseeded and finely diced
1½ teaspoons finely grated ginger
2 garlic cloves, finely chopped
seeds of ½ pomegranate
1 mango, finely diced
½ Lebanese cucumber, finely diced
1 avocado, finely diced
1 tablespoon finely chopped coriander leaves

To serve
2–4 purple or yellow witlof, leaves separated
2 limes, halved
coriander leaves

Place the fish in a large, shallow dish. Sprinkle with salt and pour over the lime juice. Leave to marinate for 5 minutes, turning once.

Whisk the olive oil and vinegar together in a small bowl to make a simple dressing.

In a large serving or salad bowl, mix the onion, chilli, ginger, garlic, pomegranate seeds, mango, cucumber, avocado and chopped coriander. Pour on the dressing and add the fish. Adjust the seasoning if needed.

To serve, place the witlof leaves on a large serving platter. Top each leaf with a spoonful of ceviche, squeeze over some lime juice and garnish with the coriander leaves.

Serves 4 as a starter

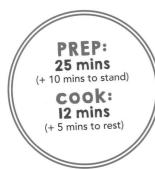

PREP:
25 mins
(+ 10 mins to stand)

COOK:
12 mins
(+ 5 mins to rest)

I am endlessly inspired by the culinary prowess of our South East Asian neighbours, particularly the incredible flavours they create with fresh herbs and aromatics. Fish sauce is one of my favourite ingredients, as it adds a delicious saltiness and fermented flavour. To balance the salt you need to add some acid in the form of lime or lemon juice or vinegar, and don't forget the chilli, garlic or ginger to round it all off. I've used banana flowers in this recipe but if you can't find any, use radishes instead. Oh, and some fermented green papaya is an awesome addition too.

BANANA FLOWER SALAD WITH CRACKLING CHICKEN

2 tablespoons lemon juice
1 large or 2 small banana flowers
100 g bean sprouts
½ green papaya, julienned
1 Lebanese cucumber, deseeded and julienned
1–2 long red chillies, deseeded and finely sliced
3 red Asian shallots, finely sliced
1 small handful of coriander leaves
1 handful of mint leaves
1 handful of Thai basil leaves
1 handful of Vietnamese mint leaves
1 handful of activated cashew nuts, toasted and chopped
1 lime, halved

Crackling chicken
4 chicken thigh fillets, skin left on
1 tablespoon sea salt
½ tablespoon coconut oil or other good-quality fat*

Dressing
1–2 small red chillies, deseeded and finely chopped
2 teaspoons finely grated ginger
2 garlic cloves, finely chopped
2 tablespoons coconut sugar*
4 tablespoons lime juice
2 tablespoons fish sauce

Crispy shallots
125 ml (½ cup) coconut oil
4 red Asian shallots, thinly sliced

See Glossary

Fill a bowl with water and add the lemon juice. Remove three or four of the purplish outer layers of the banana flowers until you get to the whitish part. Trim the stalk and the tip, then thinly slice, discarding the stamen at the base of each leaf. Place the slices in the lemon water to stop them discolouring, and leave for 10 minutes.

Meanwhile, to make the crackling chicken, pat the chicken thighs dry using paper towel and flatten with a mallet. Season the skin with salt. Melt the oil or fat in a large heavy-based frying pan over medium–high heat. Add the chicken thighs, skin-side down, and season the exposed flesh with a little salt. Fry, undisturbed, for 6–8 minutes until crispy and golden brown. Turn and cook for 3 minutes until cooked through. Transfer the chicken to a wire rack and leave to rest for 5 minutes. Chop into small pieces.

To make the dressing, place the chilli, ginger, garlic and coconut sugar in a food processor and process to a thick paste. Add the lime juice, fish sauce and process until combined.

Drain the banana flower strips and place in a large bowl. Add the bean sprouts, chicken, papaya, cucumber, chilli, shallots and herbs. Pour in the dressing, to taste, and gently toss.

To make the crispy shallots, heat the oil in a small saucepan over medium heat. Add the shallots and cook for 2½–3 minutes or until golden. Lift out with a slotted spoon and drain on paper towel. (Save the flavoured oil to use for frying and sautéing.)

Serve the salad on a platter, topped with the cashews and crispy shallots and the lime halves on the side.

Serves 4–6

PREP:
15 mins
(+ 10 mins for bread)

COOK:
5 mins
(+ 1 hr 20 mins
for bread)

Create your own version of this classic salad at home and you'll get the whole family eating their greens and good fats. Choose the type of egg (quail, duck, goose, chicken) and how you cook it (fried, poached, boiled, chopped), then the bacon (speck, prosciutto, pancetta, country ham, crispy pork belly), the green leaves (the classic cos or butter, iceberg, radicchio, rocket, cabbage, cress) and the anchovies (salted or pickled, white, chopped or whole or put through the dressing). For the crouton element we have used paleo bread. Oh, and you can also add chicken or prawns or avocado – or whatever takes your fancy really.

SIMPLE CAESAR SALAD

6 rashers of rindless bacon or pancetta (about 375 g in total)
2 baby cos lettuces, leaves separated and torn
6 marinated white anchovy fillets, rinsed and halved (optional)
2 thick slices of Nic's Paleo Bread (page 257), toasted and broken into pieces
4 soft-boiled eggs, peeled and halved

Caesar dressing
2 egg yolks
4 salted anchovy fillets, rinsed and chopped
½ garlic clove, finely chopped
1 tablespoon lemon juice
1 teaspoon Dijon mustard
250 ml (1 cup) extra-virgin olive oil
sea salt and freshly ground black pepper

To make the dressing, place the egg yolks, anchovies, garlic, lemon juice and mustard in a food processor bowl or blender jug. Process briefly until combined. With the motor running, gradually add the oil, drop by drop, until the dressing emulsifies and thickens slightly. Now pour in the oil a little faster until you have added it all and the dressing is the consistency of pouring cream. Check the seasoning, adding salt and pepper or more lemon juice, if desired. Set aside until needed.

Pan-fry the bacon or pancetta over medium–high heat for 3 minutes on each side, or until crisp and golden. Remove from the pan with tongs and drain on paper towel. When cool enough to handle, break into bite-sized pieces.

Arrange the lettuce leaves in a large serving bowl and scatter over the anchovies (if using). Top with the bacon or pancetta, toasted bread, soft-boiled eggs and drizzle over the dressing. Sprinkle with salt and pepper and serve.

Serves 4 as a main

Waldorf salad is a great family dish to make any time of year, but it's especially refreshing in the warmer months. This recipe was taught to me by Danielle Walker, author and photographer of the website Against All Grain, in her home outside San Francisco when filming for *The Paleo Way* TV series. I thoroughly recommend you look at her wonderful recipes and cookbooks. Danielle's version of this classic is pure genius and will no doubt become a staple in your own home, too.

PREP:
10 mins
(+ 5 mins for mayo)
COOK:
nil

CHICKEN WALDORF SALAD

To make the herb ranch dressing, whisk all of the ingredients together in a bowl and season. Refrigerate until ready to serve.

To serve, toss all of the ingredients together with about half of the herb ranch dressing. Leftover dressing can be stored in an airtight container in the fridge for 4–5 days.

Serves 3–4 as a main

180 g (1 cup) red grapes, halved

1½ celery stalks, thinly sliced, including a few inner leaves

1 green apple, cored and diced

50 g (½ cup) activated walnuts, chopped

2 large handfuls of mixed salad greens (such as baby spinach and rocket)

1½ cups shredded cooked chicken

Herb ranch dressing

125 g (½ cup) Mayonnaise (page 242)

3 tablespoons coconut milk

1 garlic clove, crushed

2 tablespoons chopped flat-leaf parsley leaves

1 tablespoon chopped chives

1 tablespoon chopped dill sprigs

2 teaspoons lemon juice

¼ teaspoon onion powder

sea salt

Cabbage is fast becoming a superstar in people's kitchens, and rightfully so. In its raw form, it is a powerhouse of nutrients. Fermenting it increases the bioavailability of vitamin C (Captain Cook, on his historic voyage from Britain to Australia over 200 years ago, gave his crew sauerkraut to prevent scurvy). I love to include cabbage in salads like this one. Feel free to play around with dressings, nuts, seeds and protein. To make this salad super creamy, avocado or homemade mayo work a treat, and a tablespoon or two of kraut tossed through will make it even more nutritious.

SHREDDED CABBAGE SALAD WITH WALNUTS AND SPECK

1 tablespoon coconut oil
300 g speck or rindless bacon, diced
250 g brussels sprouts, finely shredded
250 g savoy cabbage, finely shredded
1 witlof, shredded
½ pear, julienned
1 small handful of flat-leaf parsley leaves, finely chopped
1 small handful of mint leaves, finely chopped
60 g (½ cup) chopped toasted activated walnuts
sea salt and freshly ground black pepper
chilli flakes, to serve (optional)

Dijon dressing
2½ tablespoons apple cider vinegar
1 teaspoon Dijon mustard
1 teaspoon lemon zest
2 tablespoons lemon juice
½ teaspoon chilli flakes
4 tablespoons walnut oil
2 tablespoons olive oil

To make the dressing, place the vinegar, mustard, lemon zest and juice and chilli flakes in a small bowl and whisk to combine. Slowly add the walnut oil and olive oil and whisk until emulsified.

Heat the coconut oil in a large frying pan over medium–high heat. Add the speck or bacon and cook for 5 minutes, or until golden and slightly crispy. Drain on paper towel.

Combine the brussels sprouts, cabbage, witlof, pear, herbs and walnuts in a large shallow bowl and toss gently. Add the speck or bacon and the dressing and gently toss again. Season with salt and pepper and sprinkle on some chilli flakes, if desired.

Serves 4–6 as a side

When guests come over there is nothing easier than putting out a plate of smallgoods such as jamon, prosciutto, salami, ham or sausages – I always try to have some in the fridge for just such an occasion. If you want to take this idea to the next level, then serve this simple and gorgeous salad as a side or starter: your friends and family will think you were the winner of a reality TV cooking competition. Try adding some fermented veg to the salad, too.

PROSCIUTTO WITH FIG AND RADISH

To make the lemon dressing, whisk the lemon zest and juice and oil in a bowl. Season with salt and pepper and set aside until needed.

Place the fig, radish, witlof, chives, chervil and watercress in a bowl and toss lightly with the lemon dressing. Season with a little more salt and pepper, if desired.

Lay two slices of prosciutto on each serving plate, top with the salad and drizzle on some more lemon dressing.

Serves 4 as a starter

4 figs, sliced lengthways
2–3 radishes, finely sliced with a mandoline or sharp knife
2 witlof, trimmed and finely sliced
1 tablespoon finely snipped chives
a few chervil sprigs
1 large handful of watercress
8 slices of prosciutto

Lemon dressing
zest and juice of 1 lemon
4 tablespoons lemon-infused extra-virgin olive oil
sea salt and freshly ground black pepper

PREP:
10 mins (+ 20 mins for
pork scratchings)
COOK:
15 mins (+ 30 mins for
pork scratchings)

I search for inspiration all around the world and usually start with the classics, then reinterpret them to fit my paleo philosophy. This famous dish from France's beautiful city of Lyon is a simply dressed salad of frisee, soft-boiled egg and bacon that is sometimes served with croutons to add a lovely textural component. To paleo this dish, I simply replaced the croutons with pork scratchings. If you want to simplify this and still recreate the textural component, add toasted walnuts or pine nuts or pumpkin or sunflower seeds.

LYONNAISE SALAD WITH PORK SCRATCHINGS

4 rindless bacon rashers (about 250 g in total)
2 tablespoons apple cider vinegar or lemon juice
4 eggs
½ head of frisee, leaves torn
½ head of witlof, leaves torn
1 baby cos lettuce, leaves torn
1 small handful of chives, snipped into 2 cm batons
10 tarragon leaves, torn
1 large handful of chervil sprigs
sea salt and freshly ground black pepper

Pork scratchings (optional)
400 g pork rind, with at least 1 cm of fat
1½ teaspoons sea salt

Dressing
1½ tablespoons Dijon mustard
2½ tablespoons apple cider vinegar or white wine vinegar
4 tablespoons macadamia oil or olive oil
1 garlic clove, finely chopped
1 French shallot, finely chopped
sea salt and freshly ground black pepper

If you would like to make the pork scatchings, preheat the oven to 220°C. Rub the rind with the salt and set aside for 20 minutes. Cut the rind into four pieces and place, without overlapping, on a wire rack in a roasting tin. Roast in the oven, rotating the tin every 5 minutes to prevent burning, for 30 minutes, or until golden and crisp. (These are best eaten the same day, but will keep in an airtight container in the fridge for a few days.)

Pan-fry the bacon over medium–high heat for 3 minutes on each side, or until golden and crispy. Cool, then break into small pieces.

To poach the eggs, pour the vinegar or lemon juice into a saucepan of boiling salted water, then reduce the heat to medium–low so the water is just simmering. Crack an egg into a cup. Using a wooden spoon, stir the simmering water in one direction to form a whirlpool and drop the egg into the centre. Repeat with the remaining eggs and poach for 3 minutes, or until the eggs are cooked to your liking. Use a slotted spoon to remove the eggs, then drain on paper towel.

To make the dressing, combine the mustard, vinegar and 1 teaspoon of water in a bowl. Pour in the oil, in a steady stream, whisking until emulsified. Add the garlic and shallot and season well.

To make the salad, combine the frisee, witlof and cos in a large bowl. Drizzle over half of the dressing, then add the bacon and half of the herbs.

Arrange the salad on serving plates. Place the poached eggs on top, scatter around the pork scratchings (if using), garnish with the remaining herbs and season with salt and pepper. Drizzle over some more dressing, if desired.

Serves 4

PREP:
20 mins
(+ 5 mins to rest)
COOK:
2 mins

Normally the meat in this recipe is seared but it is quicker to prepare and so much more delicious and tender when the beef is served raw. If the idea of raw beef isn't to your liking, by all means, simply sear it to your desired doneness. To complete the story and bring the beef to life, add some fragrant and tantalising Asian herbs and dressing. If you want to turn this into a more substantial meal, top with a piece of grilled steak and, if you can, incorporate some fermented veg as well.

THAI BEEF SALAD

½ tablespoon sea salt
½ tablespoon freshly ground
  black pepper
450 g beef eye fillet
2 tablespoons coconut oil
1 small carrot, julienned
2 red Asian shallots, finely sliced
2 long red chillies, deseeded and
  finely sliced
1 handful of bean sprouts
3 kaffir lime leaves, finely sliced
1 small handful each of Thai basil,
  mint, coriander and Vietnamese
  mint leaves
2 tablespoons chopped activated
  cashews

Thai dressing
2 tablespoons finely diced ginger
1 tablespoon finely chopped
  coriander stalks and roots
3 garlic cloves, finely chopped
1 long red chilli, deseeded and
  finely sliced
1 tablespoon honey (optional)
2 tablespoons lime juice
1 tablespoon apple cider vinegar
2 tablespoons tamari or coconut
  aminos*
1 tablespoon finely chopped
  lemongrass, white part only
1 teaspoon sesame oil
3 tablespoons extra-virgin
  olive oil

* See Glossary

Heat a barbecue plate or chargrill pan to hot.

Sprinkle the salt and pepper on a large plate and roll the beef fillet in the seasoning to evenly coat. Lightly brush the barbecue or pan with the coconut oil and sear the beef for 30 seconds on all sides. Rest for 5 minutes, then thinly slice.

To make the dressing, combine all the ingredients in a bowl and mix well.

To serve, arrange the sliced beef on a platter and top with the carrot, shallot, chilli, bean sprouts, lime leaves and herbs. Drizzle on half of the dressing, scatter over the cashews and toss gently. Add more dressing if desired and serve chilled or at room temperature.

Serves 4

TIP

A julienne peeler is such a useful tool to have in the kitchen to speed up your veggie preparation – see page 13 for a full description.

PREP:
15 mins
(+ 2–6 hrs to marinate)

COOK:
25 mins
(+ 5 mins to rest)

The way I eat is constantly evolving and the longer I venture down the paleo path the healthier, stronger and more mentally alert I feel. Over the last couple of years I have found myself becoming fascinated by offal. Liver, brains, kidneys, tongue, heart, marrow, sweetbreads, to name just a few, are what chefs all over the world love to play with – and for good reason. Every indigenous culture has celebrated offal for what it is: a nutritional powerhouse that cannot be rivalled. Here is a simple little salad to get you started. You could of course replace heart with liver or even steak if you like, but if you can source heart I promise you will never look back.

BEEF HEART SALAD

1 beef heart (about 400 g), trimmed of sinew and gristle and cut into 4 pieces
3 tablespoons coconut oil or other good-quality fat*
1 large sweet potato (about 400 g), cut into 1 cm cubes
sea salt and freshly ground black pepper
1 handful of chervil sprigs, torn
1 handful of flat-leaf parsley leaves, torn
½ French shallot, finely chopped
1 large handful of baby spinach leaves
1 large handful of wild rocket leaves
2 hard-boiled eggs, peeled and grated

Marinade
125 ml (½ cup) balsamic vinegar or coconut aminos*
160 ml (scant ⅔ cup) apple cider vinegar
8 thyme sprigs
1 teaspoon peppercorns, crushed
3 garlic cloves, crushed, skin on

Dressing
2 tablespoons white wine vinegar or apple cider vinegar
1 tablespoon finely chopped flat-leaf parsley leaves
pinch of ground cumin
3 tablespoons extra-virgin olive oil

* See Glossary

To make the marinade, combine all of the ingredients in a bowl with 100 ml of water. Pour over the beef heart, cover and marinate in the fridge for 2–6 hours.

Half an hour before the beef is marinated, preheat the oven to 200°C. Grease a baking tray with a little coconut oil or fat.

Place the sweet potato on the prepared tray, drizzle over 1 tablespoon of oil or fat and toss to evenly coat. Season with salt and pepper. Cover with foil and roast for 12–15 minutes, or until tender. Remove the foil and cook for a further 2 minutes until lightly golden. Set aside, keeping warm.

Meanwhile, remove the heart from the marinade and heat a barbecue plate or chargrill pan to medium–hot. Rub the remaining oil or fat over the heart and season with salt and pepper. Cook for 3–4 minutes on each side for medium–rare (or cook to your liking). Cover with foil and leave to rest for 5 minutes before slicing.

To make the salsa, combine the chervil, parsley, shallot, sweet potato, spinach and rocket in a bowl.

In another bowl, make the dressing by mixing all of the ingredients together.

Pour just enough dressing over the salsa to coat. Toss gently and season with salt and pepper. Arrange the salsa on a large platter or serving plates, top with the beef heart and the egg and drizzle on some more dressing.

Serves 4

Steak tartare is in my top ten dishes of all time and would feature in my last supper. The key is to use the best grass-fed and finished beef or lamb and finely dice it. If you want to add heart — and tartare is a wonderful way to try it — you need to dice it super fine or put it through a mincer. Add your seasoning, spices and sauces to match the cuisine you want to try (French, Italian, Japanese, South American, Vietnamese, Indian, etc.) and you are done. Here is a Korean version that is served on sesame leaves, but you could use cabbage or lettuce leaves or even thin slices of cucumber or raw daikon.

PREP:
15 mins
COOK:
nil

KOREAN STEAK TARTARE WITH KIMCHI AND NASHI

For the dressing, combine all the ingredients in a bowl and whisk well.

To make the tartare, combine the beef, spring onion, pine nuts and dressing in a bowl and mix well. Season with a little salt and pepper.

Place the sesame leaves on a large platter, spread some Korean chilli paste on each leaf, then top with slices of nashi pear and a couple of spoonfuls of tartare. Drizzle on some egg yolk and sprinkle on the sesame seeds. Serve with the kimchi on the side.

Serves 4

500 g beef eye fillet or sirloin, finely chopped
2 spring onions, finely chopped
2 tablespoons pine nuts, toasted
8 sesame leaves (see note)
2 teaspoons fermented chilli paste or sugar-free chilli sauce
1 nashi pear, finely sliced
2 egg yolks, beaten
black and white sesame seeds, toasted, to serve
kimchi, to serve

Dressing
3 tablespoons tamari or coconut aminos*
1 tablespoon honey
1 garlic clove, finely chopped
3 teaspoons sesame oil
pinch each of sea salt and freshly ground black pepper
2 tablespoons apple cider vinegar
2 teaspoons fermented chilli paste or sugar-free chilli sauce

See Glossary

Note
Sesame leaves look similar to Japanese shiso leaves (see glossary) but have a stronger flavour. They are available from Asian grocers.

Carpaccio is a delicious dish of thinly sliced raw beef — usually fillet or sirloin — seasoned with olive oil, lemon juice, salt and pepper and that is about it. Celeriac remoulade, a combination of thinly sliced celeriac and mustard mayonnaise, is to die for and works well on its own; however, when you pair it with carpaccio all nutritional bases are covered and you get this amazing textural experience from the aioli, the crunchy celeriac and the melt-in-your-mouth beef.

BEEF CARPACCIO WITH CELERIAC REMOULADE

4 beef tenderloins (about 70 g each)
2 tablespoons extra-virgin olive oil, plus extra to serve
1 lemon, halved
sea salt and freshly ground black pepper
1 large handful of wild rocket leaves
1 teaspoon snipped chives, to serve
1 small handful of chervil sprigs, to serve
finely grated fresh horseradish, to serve

Celeriac remoulade
⅓ celeriac (about 200 g), julienned
2 teaspoons wholegrain mustard
2 tablespoons chopped flat-leaf parsley leaves
4 tablespoons Aioli (page 242)
1 teaspoon truffle-infused olive oil (optional)
sea salt and freshly ground black pepper

To make the celeriac remoulade, combine all the ingredients in a bowl.

Place one piece of beef between two sheets of plastic wrap and pound with a meat mallet until 2 mm thick. Remove the top layer of plastic wrap, flip over onto a serving plate and remove the remaining layer of plastic wrap. Drizzle over 2 teaspoons of the olive oil and a squeeze of lemon juice. Gently rub in with your fingertips. Repeat this process with the remaining beef, olive oil and lemon juice. Season with some salt and pepper.

For each serving, use 2 tablespoons to shape a large spoonful of celeriac remoulade into a quenelle and place on the beef. Scatter over one-quarter each of the rocket, chives and chervil, then drizzle with some extra olive oil. Finish with some grated horseradish.

Serves 4 as a starter

MAKE A BIG BATCH AND ENJOY THE NEXT DAY!

Add fermented veg to every meal for good gut health

MAIN MEALS

Fresh ingredients, cooked simply and without fuss

Soups
Burgers
Curries
Skewers
Roasts

PREP:
15 mins
(+ 20 mins to marinate)

cook:
28 mins

The key with all meat-based soups is to start with a nutrient-rich stock made from simmering bones of choice, which, in this instance, would be fish bones or seafood shells. Once you have the stock (I recommend you make it in bulk and freeze so you have some on hand at all times), then it is as simple as adding aromatics, some vegetables and protein. I used fish here, but you could try mussels, clams, prawns, scallops, squid or anything you love. I have a feeling that this will become a favourite soup for special occasions.

SPICY FISH SOUP

1 kg snapper fillets (or other firm white fish), skin left on and cut into 4 cm pieces
2 tablespoons lime juice
2 teaspoons sea salt
1.3 litres fish stock or water
3 lemongrass stems, white part only, bruised
350 g sweet potato, cut into 2.5 cm cubes
6 kaffir lime leaves
200 g Chinese broccoli (gai larn), roughly chopped
3 tomatoes, cut into wedges
2 teaspoons tamarind* puree
1 tablespoon coconut sugar*
freshly ground white pepper
coriander leaves, to serve

Spice paste
2 teaspoons coriander seeds, toasted and crushed
2 red Asian shallots, chopped
4 long red chillies, deseeded and roughly chopped
½ bird's eye chilli, deseeded and roughly chopped
2 lemongrass stems, white part only, roughly chopped
2 tablespoons finely grated galangal*
1 tablespoon chopped fresh turmeric or 1 teaspoon ground turmeric
2 tablespoons chopped coriander roots
3 teaspoons grated ginger
½ teaspoon shrimp paste*

* See Glossary

Place the fish in a bowl and coat evenly with the lime juice and salt. Cover and leave to marinate in the fridge for 20 minutes.

To make the spice paste, place all the ingredients in a food processor bowl and blend with 3 tablespoons of water until smooth. Add a little more water if the paste is too thick. Set aside.

Pour the fish stock or water into a large saucepan and bring to the boil. Add the spice paste, lemongrass, sweet potato and lime leaves and simmer for 15 minutes. Add the Chinese broccoli and simmer for a further 5 minutes. Add the marinated fish and any juices from the bowl, the tomato, tamarind puree and sugar. Reduce the heat to low and gently simmer for 6–8 minutes, or until the fish is just cooked through and the vegetables are tender. Season with salt and white pepper.

Ladle the fish soup into serving bowls and garnish with the coriander leaves.

Serves 6

This wonderfully nourishing soup balances hot and sour flavours that dance on the tongue. Have a play around with different vegetables and animal proteins. This soup works well with seafood, beef, pork, chicken, duck or lamb. Remember to make extra so you can have it the next day for breakfast or pack it in a thermos for lunch.

HOT AND SOUR SOUP

4 tablespoons tamari or coconut aminos*

3 tablespoons apple cider vinegar

1 tablespoon toasted sesame oil

1 teaspoon honey

1 tablespoon coconut oil or other good-quality fat*

2 red Asian shallots, finely diced

4 cm piece of ginger, peeled and grated

1 teaspoon finely chopped coriander root

1 long red chilli, deseeded and chopped

500 g pork loin, cut into thin strips

12 fresh wood ear fungus (about 40 g), sliced (see note)

4 fresh shiitake mushrooms (about 60 g), sliced

100 g bamboo shoots, sliced

2 kaffir lime leaves, torn

2 litres (8 cups) chicken stock

2½ tablespoons tapioca flour*

3 eggs, whisked

sea salt

1 spring onion, finely sliced on the diagonal

See Glossary

Note
Brown and ear-shaped, wood ear fungus are commonly used in Chinese cuisine. They are available from Asian grocers.

Mix the tamari or coconut aminos, vinegar, sesame oil and honey together in a bowl and set aside until needed.

Heat the oil or fat in a large saucepan over medium–high heat. Add the shallot, ginger, coriander root and chilli and cook for 2 minutes until softened and fragrant. Add the pork and cook, stirring occasionally, for 3 minutes until the meat starts to colour. Add the wood ears, shiitake mushrooms, bamboo shoots, kaffir lime leaves and 1 litre of the stock and simmer for 10 minutes. Stir in the tamari mixture.

Mix the tapioca flour with the remaining stock and stir into the soup. Continue to simmer until the soup thickens slightly, about 3 minutes.

Slowly pour the whisked eggs into the soup in a steady stream while gently stirring. Simmer for 30 seconds until the eggs are cooked and look stringy. Add some salt, if needed, and if you prefer your soup to be quite sour, add a little more vinegar. Ladle the soup into serving bowls and garnish with the spring onion.

Serves 6

We all know broccoli is a nutritional powerhouse – high in vitamin K and vitamin C – but it tastes bloody good, too. I love it either raw or cooked in salads; roasted until it goes crispy around the edges and then tossed in a garlic and apple cider vinegar dressing; and in stir-fries and curries to soak up the sauce. I have included this simple soup as it's a great way to use broccoli when it's in season and the price is low. You can make a huge batch and freeze it in containers, then add your protein of choice (I have used smoked trout here) or poach an egg in it.

PREP:
15 mins
COOK:
20 mins

BROCCOLI SOUP WITH WILD TROUT

Heat the oil or fat in a saucepan over medium–high heat. Add the onion and cook for 5 minutes until translucent. Add the broccoli stems and garlic and cook, stirring occasionally, for 5 minutes until starting to brown.

Add the broccoli florets, rosemary and dill to the pan, then pour in the stock and bring to the boil. Reduce the heat to low and simmer for 10–15 minutes, or until the broccoli is tender. Season with salt and pepper.

Using a hand-held blender, blend the soup until it is thick and chunky.

Ladle the soup into serving bowls, then top with the flaked trout, toasted seeds and a sprinkling of lemon zest. Serve hot.

Serves 4

2 tablespoons coconut oil or other good-quality fat*
1 onion, chopped
2 heads of broccoli (about 600 g), broken into florets, stems chopped
2 garlic cloves, finely chopped
1 tablespoon finely chopped rosemary leaves
1 tablespoon finely chopped dill, plus extra to garnish
750 ml (3 cups) chicken, fish or vegetable stock, or water
sea salt and freshly ground black pepper
240 g hot-smoked trout, skin and bones removed, flesh flaked
1 tablespoons sunflower seeds, toasted
1 tablespoon pumpkin seeds, toasted
finely grated zest of 1 lemon

* See Glossary

PREP:
15 mins
(+ 12 mins for buns)
COOK:
5 mins
(+ 1 hr for buns)

I often travel to the Northern Territory to go fishing, and have noticed that many restaurants and eating houses there have barramundi burgers on the menu. In honour of one of my favourite places to visit, I thought it only fitting that I recreate a paleo version of the 'barra' burger. Get the freshest wild fish fillets you can, then make a kick-ass tartare sauce, toast your paleo buns and fill them with lettuce and a squeeze of lemon – and you are laughing. Fold some sauerkraut into the tartare sauce to make it a probiotic powerhouse.

CRUMBED FISH BURGERS WITH ARTICHOKE TARTARE SAUCE

200 g (2 cups) almond meal
zest of 1 lemon
1 tablespoon finely chopped
    flat-leaf parsley
80 g (heaped ½ cup) tapioca
    flour*
2 eggs, lightly beaten
700 g firm white fish fillets of
    your choice (such as barramundi,
    snapper or whiting), skinned
    and pin-boned, cut into burger
    bun-sized pieces
200 ml coconut oil or other
    good-quality fat*
lemon wedges, to serve
6 Paleo Buns (page 248)
6 baby cos leaves

Artichoke tartare sauce
2 egg yolks
1 garlic clove, finely chopped
1 teaspoon Dijon mustard
juice of 1 lemon
150 ml olive oil or macadamia oil
4 small marinated artichoke
    hearts, drained and finely
    chopped
10 flat-leaf parsley leaves, finely
    chopped
2 tablespoons salted baby
    capers, rinsed well, patted dry
    and finely chopped
sea salt and freshly ground
    black pepper

* See Glossary

To make the artichoke tartare sauce, place the egg yolks, garlic, mustard and lemon juice in a food processor bowl and process to combine. With the motor running, slowly add the oil in a thin stream, until thick and emulsified. Transfer to a bowl, stir through the artichoke, parsley and capers and season with salt and pepper.

Combine the almond meal, lemon zest and parsley in a shallow bowl. Place the tapioca flour in another shallow bowl and the eggs in a third bowl. Lightly season the fish with some salt, then dust with the tapioca flour, coat with the egg and, lastly, firmly press on the almond meal mixture.

Heat the oil or fat in a large frying pan over medium–high heat. Fry the crumbed fish in batches for 45–60 seconds on each side until golden and cooked through. Drain on paper towel. Season with a little more salt and squeeze some lemon on top.

Cut the paleo buns in half. Place a cos leaf on each bun base, then add the crumbed fish and a dollop of artichoke tartare sauce. Top with the other half of the bun and serve.

Serves 6

Growing up on Queensland's Gold Coast, my weekends were pretty simple. I would head to the beach at 5am on my trusty pushbike with my surfboard under my arm and return home at 5pm absolutely worn out from a day of surfing, riding and playing with my mates. Around lunchtime I would head to the local milk bar and order a simple but utterly delicious steak sanga of toasted bread with a thin piece of steak, some mayo, caramelised onion, tomato, lettuce, salt and pepper and tomato sauce. I wanted to recreate a paleo version of this classic steak sanga to bring back my childhood memories.

MY STEAK SANGA

4 × 120 g beef steaks (such as sirloin, flank, skirt, rump or scotch steaks), lightly pounded with a mallet
2 tablespoons coconut oil or other good-quality fat*
1 onion, sliced
sea salt and freshly ground black pepper
8 slices of Nic's Paleo Bread (page 257), toasted
2 tablespoons good-quality, sugar-free tomato ketchup
1 large tomato, sliced
1 large handful of rocket leaves
4 tablespoons Mayonnaise (page 242)

Marinade
2 garlic cloves, finely chopped
4 tablespoons duck fat, melted
2 tablespoons sherry vinegar or apple cider vinegar
3 tablespoons Worcestershire sauce
¾ teaspoon freshly ground black pepper
1 tablespoon fresh or dried thyme leaves

See Glossary

To make the marinade, place all the ingredients in a bowl and mix well. Place the steaks in the dish and turn to evenly coat. Cover with plastic wrap and place in the fridge for at least 2 hours or, for best results, overnight.

Drain the meat and discard the marinade. Allow the meat to come to room temperature, about 20 minutes.

Heat a barbecue plate or chargrill pan to medium–hot. Brush with the oil or fat. Add the onion and cook for 6–8 minutes until translucent and lightly caramelised. While the onion is cooking, season the steaks with some salt and cook for 1–1½ minutes on each side for medium–rare (or cook to your liking). Cover with foil and allow to rest for a couple of minutes.

To assemble the steak sandwiches, spread four slices of toast with tomato ketchup. Add a slice or two of tomato, then the steak, some caramelised onion and rocket and a drizzle of mayonnaise. Top with the remaining toast, cut in half and enjoy.

Serves 4

I feel that it is only fitting that I include a paleo version of Australia's beloved prawn roll, so no one has to feel like they are missing out. There really isn't anything restrictive about the paleo way of eating; in fact, it is more about celebrating nourishing food. The paleo bun recipe was taught to me by Josef from Sprout Cafe in Dubbo, and I can't thank him enough for sharing it with me and you.

PREP:
10 mins
(+ 5 mins for aioli,
10 mins for tomato relish
& 12 mins for buns)
cook:
nil (+1 hr for buns)

PRAWN ROLLS

Combine the prawns, celery, aioli, tomato relish, tarragon and lemon juice in a bowl, stir and season with salt and pepper.

Slice the buns in half without cutting all the way through. Place some lettuce in each bun, then top with the prawn mixture.

Serves 4

350 g cooked and shelled prawns
1 celery stalk, finely sliced
160 g Aioli (page 242)
4 tablespoons Tomato Relish
   (page 255)
1 handful of tarragon leaves (or
   flat-leaf parsley, basil, chives)
juice of ½ lemon
sea salt and freshly ground black
   pepper
4 Paleo Buns (page 248)
1 large handful of iceberg lettuce
   leaves, torn

PREP:
10 mins
(+ 5 mins for mayo,
5 mins for chimichurri
& 10 mins for bread)
cook:
15 mins (+ 1 hr
20 mins for bread)

Finding a great paleo bread recipe is often all the inspiration people need to take the plunge and adopt a paleo lifestyle. And what better way to use paleo bread than to make the mother of all sandwiches – the club sanga. The classic flavour combinations work so well: crispy bacon, roasted chicken or turkey, lettuce, tomato and mayonnaise. I have included egg and avocado as well, and don't forget some fermented veggies like kraut on the side.

PALEO CLUB SANGA

4 tablespoons Mayonnaise
(page 242)
1 tablespoon Chimichurri
(page 251)
2 chicken breast fillets or
4 thigh fillets
2 tablespoons coconut oil or
other good-quality fat*, melted
sea salt and freshly ground
black pepper
4 rashers of rindless bacon
4 eggs
12 slices of Nic's Paleo Bread
(page 257), toasted
8 cos lettuce leaves
1 avocado, sliced
1 tomato, sliced

* See Glossary

Combine the mayonnaise and chimichurri in a bowl and mix well. Set aside until needed.

Coat the chicken in the oil or fat and season with salt and pepper.

Heat a large frying pan over medium–high heat. Add the chicken and cook for 3–4 minutes on each side until lightly golden and cooked through. Transfer to a plate, cover with foil and keep warm.

Return the pan to medium–high heat. Add the bacon and cook for 3 minutes on each side until crisp. Transfer to the plate with the chicken, cover and keep warm.

Place the pan over medium–high heat again. Add a little oil or fat if needed, then crack in the eggs and cook for 2 minutes until the whites are set and the yolks are still runny. Season the eggs with a little salt and pepper, then flip over and cook for a further 10 seconds to seal. Remove from the heat and keep warm.

Cut the chicken into thin slices.

To assemble, spread eight slices of toast with the chimichurri mayonnaise. Layer the cos lettuce, chicken and avocado on four of them. Follow with another slice of bread with chimichurri mayonnaise, then add a slice of tomato, some bacon and an egg. Top with the remaining bread slices, cut the sandwiches in half and insert a wooden skewer in the centre to hold the layers in place.

Serves 4

PREP:
15 mins
(+ 5 mins for mayo
& 10 mins for buns)

COOK:
10 mins
(+ 1 hr for buns)

A lot of people ask me how to get their family to eat paleo. My answer is always the same: 'Don't tell 'em and just cook this delicious food.' There's no need to make a big deal about paleo, just get your family involved in the shopping and cooking and then enjoy eating what you've prepared. This burger recipe will make even the most paleo-resistant person change their mind about this way of eating. Go nuts with the toppings or keep it simple. Also, try adding some fermented gherkins or veg to the burger or on the side.

BURGER WITH THE LOT

4 tablespoons coconut oil or
   other good-quality fat*, melted
4 rashers of rindless bacon
   (optional)
2 onions, sliced into thin rings
4 eggs
4 Paleo Buns (page 248), halved
8 slices of tomato
2 carrots, grated
1 large beetroot, cooked
   and sliced
8 butter lettuce leaves
good-quality tomato ketchup,
   to serve
wholegrain mustard, to serve
Mayonnaise (page 242)

Patties
600 g minced beef
½ onion, finely diced
2 garlic cloves, crushed
1 egg
pinch of chilli flakes
1 tablespoon chopped
   flat-leaf parsley
pinch of dried oregano
1 teaspoon each of sea salt and
   freshly ground black pepper

* See Glossary

To make the patties, combine all of the ingredients in a large bowl and mix well. Shape into four patties.

Heat a barbecue plate or chargrill pan to medium–high. Brush with 2 tablespoons of the oil or fat, add the patties, bacon (if using) and onion and cook, stirring the onion occasionally so that it doesn't burn, for 5 minutes. Turn the patties and bacon and continue to cook for a couple of minutes until the patties are cooked through, the bacon is crisp and the onion is caramelised. Remove from the barbecue and keep warm.

Heat the remaining oil or fat on the barbecue and cook the eggs for 2 minutes until the whites are set and the yolks are still runny. Season the eggs with a little salt and pepper, then flip over and cook for a further 10 seconds to seal. Remove from the heat and keep warm.

Arrange the patties, paleo buns, onion, eggs and bacon (if using) on a serving platter and place in the centre of the table. Place the tomato, carrot, beetroot, lettuce, tomato ketchup, mustard and mayonnaise in bowls and let everyone build their own burger.

Serves 4

Barbecue ideas in a flash

For an **easy barbecued mushroom dish**, place some coconut oil, parsley leaves, anchovy fillets and garlic cloves in a food processor and process until smooth. Spoon the paste into some large mushrooms, gill-side up. Wrap each mushroom in foil and then cook on the barbecue for 10 minutes, or until cooked through.

The best cuts of beef to throw on the barbecue are eye fillet, scotch fillet, rib eye, porterhouse, T-bone and rump. Beef liver, heart and marrow are also brilliant on the barbie. Always look for cuts with a little fat marbled through the meat, as this helps the steak to stay moist and tender.

To make some super-quick skewers for the barbie, combine a little lemon juice, dried oregano, honey and crushed garlic in a bowl and toss cubes of lamb through it. Thread the lamb onto skewers with some capsicum, mushrooms and tomatoes, then brush with some oil. Cook on a medium–high barbecue for about 10 minutes, turning every 2 minutes, or until cooked to your liking. Serve with beetroot chimichurri (page 251).

To make a simple spice rub for your meat, grind some peppercorns and coriander seeds using a mortar and pestle or spice grinder. Stir through some salt and garlic powder. Rub a little coconut oil over your meat, then sprinkle on the spice rub and barbecue to your liking.

QUICK MARINADES

Teriyaki marinade – particularly great for chicken and pork.
Mix tamari or coconut aminos, water, Worcestershire sauce, honey, apple cider vinegar, coconut oil, onion powder, garlic powder and grated ginger.
Greek marinade – best with lamb but good on any meat.
Mix lemon juice, tallow, garlic, thyme, oregano and bay leaf.
Ginger, honey and tamari marinade – delicious with any kind of poultry.
Mix ginger, honey, tamari or coconut aminos, sesame seeds and chilli powder.
Korean bulgogi marinade – use with thinly cut strips of beef.
Mix tamari or coconut aminos, sesame oil, honey, garlic, shallots, sesame seeds and black pepper.
Mexican fajita marinade – use with chicken or beef.
Mix lime juice, coconut oil, honey, chilli powder, smoked paprika, garlic and pepper.

One of my favourite ways to prepare zucchini for the barbecue is to slice it thinly lengthways, brush with coconut oil and sprinkle with Italian seasoning and salt. Pop the zucchini slices onto the barbie and cook for 3–4 minutes on each side, or until starting to brown. Brush with a little balsamic vinegar and cook for another minute. Finish with a drizzle of olive oil and serve.

Sardines really should feature more on people's tables. Aside from the awesome health benefits of their calcium, omega 3s and other goodies, sardines are a sustainable seafood. This recipe is a great way to introduce your family to sardines: grilled on the barbecue with a delicious marinade, and served with a gorgeous crisp salad and some fermented veg.

PREP:
10 mins
COOK:
3 mins

GRILLED SARDINES WITH CHILLI, OREGANO AND LEMON

To make the marinade, mix the coconut oil with the dried and fresh oregano, chilli flakes, parsley, lemon zest, garlic and some salt and pepper.

Brush the marinade over the sardines.

Heat a barbecue plate or chargrill pan to hot. Cook the sardines on each side for 40–60 seconds until just cooked through. Drizzle over some of the remaining marinade, scatter on the oregano leaves and serve with the lemon wedges and a salad of your choice.

Serves 2–4

10 whole sardines (about 500 g in total), cleaned and rinsed (ask your fishmonger to do this)
oregano leaves, to serve
lemon wedges, to serve

Marinade
120 ml (scant ½ cup) coconut oil, melted
2 tablespoons dried oregano
2 tablespoons chopped oregano leaves
1 teaspoon chilli flakes
2 tablespoons chopped flat-leaf parsley leaves
finely grated zest of 1 lemon
1 garlic clove, finely chopped
sea salt and freshly ground black pepper

Tip

This marinade is also great with any type of fish, shellfish, chicken, steak or anything else that you like to throw on the barbie.

Spices can transform the humblest of ingredients into superstars. Jamaican jerk spice, a favourite of mine, combines thyme and garlic and some of the world's most intoxicating and addictive spices — allspice, cloves, cinnamon and nutmeg — with the heat from chillies. Try adding this spice mix to your next meatloaf or bolognese, or rub it onto a chicken before roasting.

ROASTED TROUT WITH JERK SPICE GLAZE

6 trout fillets (about 180 g each), skin left on, pin-boned
melted coconut oil, for brushing
Herb and Anchovy Dressing (page 253)

Jerk spice glaze
3 spring onions, finely chopped
2 garlic cloves, finely chopped
1 habanero or Scotch bonnet chilli, deseeded and finely chopped
3 tablespoons molasses
2 tablespoons coconut sugar*
2 tablespoons tamari
1½ tablespoons coconut oil, melted
1½ tablespoons dark rum (optional)
½ tablespoon lemon juice
½ tablespoon dried thyme
½ teaspoon ground allspice
¼ teaspoon ground cinnamon
pinch of freshly grated nutmeg
½ teaspoon sea salt
¼ teaspoon freshly ground black pepper

See Glossary

Position a rack in the centre of the oven and preheat the oven to 200°C. Line a baking tray with foil and brush with coconut oil.

To make the jerk spice glaze, place all of the ingredients in a food processor bowl and pulse until blended. Pour the mixture into a small bowl and set aside.

Pat each trout fillet dry with paper towel, then season with salt and pepper. Place the trout, skin-side down, on the prepared tray. Generously brush the top of the trout with the jerk spice glaze, then roast for 6–8 minutes, or until the flesh is tender and opaque.

Place a piece of trout on each serving plate and top with 2 tablespoons of herb and anchovy dressing. Serve with your favourite salad.

Serves 6

Cooking is an essential life skill and I believe it should be taught to every child at school so they have the tools to create nutrient-dense dishes that will keep them healthy throughout life. Once you know the basics, you can pretty much reinterpret any recipe so that you never need cook the same dish twice. Take this recipe, for example. It is based on the Italian classic osso buco, but I've swapped veal for the most under appreciated and under utilised part of a fish – the wings. If you can't buy fish wings from your fishmonger, simply use fillets, a whole fish or even prawns or lobster.

FISH WINGS 'OSSO BUCO'

3 tablespoons coconut oil or other good-quality fat*
8 fish wings (try barramundi or kingfish)
sea salt and freshly ground black pepper
120 g pancetta, finely diced
1 celery stalk, finely chopped
1 onion, finely chopped
2 garlic cloves, finely chopped
1 tablespoon thyme leaves
1 carrot, finely diced
1½ tablespoons tomato paste
3 anchovy fillets, finely chopped
250 ml (1 cup) dry white wine
6 Roma tomatoes, roughly chopped
1 handful of flat-leaf parsley, finely chopped
finely grated zest of 1 lemon

See Glossary

Preheat the oven to 180°C.

In a deep ovenproof frying pan large enough to hold the fish in a single layer, heat 1 tablespoon of oil or fat over medium–high heat. Season the fish wings with salt and pepper and seal on both sides for 1 minute until light golden. Transfer to a dish and set aside.

Wipe the pan clean and heat the remaining oil over medium heat. Add the pancetta and cook for 2 minutes, or until lightly golden. Add the celery, onion, garlic, thyme and carrot and cook, stirring occasionally, for 3 minutes until the vegetables have softened. Stir through the tomato paste, anchovies, wine and tomatoes. Bring to the boil, then reduce the heat to low and gently simmer for 15 minutes. Season with salt and pepper.

Place the fish wings back in the pan and arrange them in a single layer to ensure they cook evenly. Add 180 ml of water, cover with a lid and cook in the oven for 10 minutes.

To serve, place the wings on a large serving plate, spoon the sauce over the top, then garnish with the parsley and lemon zest.

Serves 4

It is awesome to eat 'real food' at breakfast. What do I mean by real food? Well, the food you would normally eat at dinner — soups, curries, roasts, etc. Not so long ago, farmers considered steak and eggs a normal way to start the day. Other cultures around the world eat real food for breakfast, not boring cereal or toast concoctions. Here I've modified a breakfast called shrimp and grits from the southern parts of the United States. Originally made with corn, I have used cauliflower for the grits because it has an amazing texture and flavour. Give this a try for breakfast — or lunch or dinner. It's perfect for any time of the day really.

PREP:
15 mins
COOK:
25 mins

PRAWNS AND GRITS

To make the grits, place the cauliflower in a food processor bowl and pulse a few times into tiny pieces that resemble grains of rice. Melt the coconut oil in a saucepan over medium–high heat, add the onion and cook, stirring occasionally, for 5 minutes until softened. Add the garlic and cook for 30 seconds, then stir in the cauliflower rice and chicken stock and bring to the boil. Reduce the heat to low, mix in the almond meal and simmer, stirring occasionally, for 15 minutes until nice and thick. Season with salt and pepper. Drizzle on some olive oil and fold in. Set aside and keep warm.

While the grits are cooking, heat the oil in a non-stick frying pan over medium heat. Add the bacon and cook for 3 minutes on each side until crisp. If you like your bacon very crisp, cook for longer. Remove from the pan and chop or break into small pieces. Set aside and keep warm. Leave the bacon fat in the pan for cooking the prawns.

Combine the prawn spice seasoning ingredients in a bowl. Add the prawns, tossing to coat evenly.

Place the pan with the bacon fat over medium–high heat. Add the prawns and seal for 1 minute on each side. Remove from the pan and set aside. Add the onion and cook, stirring occasionally, for 5 minutes until softened. Add the garlic, tomato and chilli and cook for 3 minutes, until the tomato has broken down. Add the stock, bring to a simmer and cook for a further 2 minutes. Return the prawns to the pan and cook for 2 minutes until cooked through. Season with salt and pepper.

Serve the prawns on top of the cauliflower grits with a sprinkle of bacon chips and oregano leaves.

Serves 4

1 tablespoon coconut oil
4 rashers of rindless bacon
12 raw king prawns, shelled and deveined, tails left intact
1 onion, chopped
3 garlic cloves, finely chopped
2 tomatoes, chopped
1 long red chilli, deseeded and finely chopped
185 ml (¾ cup) chicken stock or water
oregano leaves, to serve

Cauliflower grits
1 cauliflower (about 700 g), florets and stalk roughly chopped
1 tablespoon coconut oil
½ onion, finely chopped
1 garlic clove, finely chopped
625 ml (2½ cups) chicken stock or water
100 g (1 cup) almond meal
sea salt and freshly ground black pepper
2 tablespoons olive oil

Prawn spice seasoning
1 teaspoon paprika
½ teaspoon dried oregano
¼ teaspoon chilli flakes

PREP:
10 mins
(+ 5 mins for aioli)
COOK:
18 mins

We all love the simple things in life: a walk along the beach with loved ones, laughing at a silly movie and eating fresh ingredients cooked simply and without fuss. All you need are the basics: a couple of beautiful vegetables that work well with fish, such as fennel and zucchini; a little sweetness from dried fruit; some crunch from nuts; and some good-quality fat in the form of mayo or aioli. And there you have it! For variety, you can substitute the fish fillets for chicken thigh fillets, lamb chops or steak and you will have an awesome meal at any time.

BARBECUED FISH WITH FENNEL, ZUCCHINI AND CURRANTS

2 tablespoons coconut oil or other good-quality fat*, plus extra to rub
1 large fennel bulb, finely sliced
1 zucchini, finely sliced lengthways
2 tablespoons pine nuts
2 tablespoons currants
2 tablespoons sultanas
1 teaspoon finely snipped chives
sea salt and freshly ground black pepper
4 firm white fish fillets (about 150 g each), skin left on
3 tablespoons extra-virgin olive oil, to serve
1 lemon, halved
4 tablespoons Aioli (page 242), to serve

See Glossary

Heat the oil or fat in a large frying pan over medium–high heat. Add the fennel and zucchini and sauté for 1 minute, tossing frequently. Throw in the pine nuts, currants, sultanas and chives and sauté for 30 seconds until the vegetables are just tender. Season with salt and pepper.

Heat a barbecue plate or chargrill pan to high. Season the fish with salt and pepper and rub both sides with the extra oil or fat. Place the fillets, skin-side up, on the barbecue, cover with foil and cook until golden brown, about 4 minutes. Remove the foil, flip the fillets over with a spatula and cook until the fish is completely opaque throughout, at least 6 minutes.

Place the fish on a platter or on serving plates with the sautéed fennel mixture. Drizzle on some olive oil, then squeeze some lemon juice over the top. Serve with aioli on the side.

Serves 4

TIPS

I love using barramundi fillets for this recipe, but cod, Spanish mackerel, trevalla, mulloway and pink snapper also work really well.

A mandoline is really helpful for this recipe, to slice the fennel and zucchini thinly. If you don't have one, make sure you use a really sharp knife.

This is basically a cooked version of the South American dish ceviche. The classic ingredients of coconut milk, lime, onion, tomato, chilli and coriander are simmered in a gut-healing fish stock and teamed with cauliflower, broccoli or zucchini rice to make a wonderfully flavourful dish. Serve with a delicious salad and some fermented veg for even better gut health.

BRAZILIAN FISH STEW

1 kg snapper or other white-fleshed fish fillets, skinned and cut into 5 cm pieces
3 tablespoons lime juice
sea salt and freshly ground black pepper
3 tablespoons coconut oil
1½ onions, 1 onion diced, ½ onion thinly sliced
8 garlic cloves, finely chopped
2 Roma tomatoes, 1 tomato chopped, the other thinly sliced
250 ml (1 cup) fish stock or water
250 ml (1 cup) coconut cream
1 long red chilli, deseeded and finely chopped
1 tablespoon chopped coriander leaves, plus extra leaves to garnish
2 limes, halved, to serve
Cauliflower or Zucchini Rice (page 208), to serve

Place the fish and lime juice in a bowl and season with salt and pepper. Cover and place in the fridge to marinate for 10 minutes.

Meanwhile, heat the coconut oil in a saucepan over medium heat. Add the diced onion and cook for 4 minutes until softened, then add the garlic and cook for 30 seconds until fragrant. Stir in the chopped tomato and cook until broken down, about 5 minutes. Pour in the stock and coconut cream and bring to the boil.

Drain the fish (discard the lime juice) and add it to the simmering coconut soup. Reduce the heat to low, cover the pan and cook the fish for 5 minutes until almost cooked through. Add the chilli, coriander, sliced tomato and sliced onion and cook for 2 minutes. Season with salt and pepper.

Ladle the fish stew into serving bowls. Garnish with the coriander leaves and squeeze on some lime juice to finish. Serve with some cauliflower or zucchini rice on the side.

Serves 4–6

For me, catching, cooking and eating whole fish is one of life's greatest pleasures. When I can't catch my own I try to buy my fish whole because it's usually a lot fresher and retains more moisture than fillets. I also love to use the bones and heads to make my own stock. This recipe uses a wonderful marinade that really takes the fish to another level, and the addition of green olives puts this dish among my favourites in the book. Serve with fermented vegetables and maybe a fresh cucumber or fennel salad on the side.

PREP:
10 mins
COOK:
7 mins

BARBECUED MOROCCAN FLOUNDER

Heat a barbecue plate or large chargrill pan to medium–hot.

To make the marinade, combine the parsley, coriander, garlic, vinegar, chilli, paprika and saffron in a food processor bowl, then process until finely chopped. With the motor running, slowly add the coconut oil until combined. Season with salt and pepper.

Place the fish on a large plate, pour on the marinade, then turn to coat evenly. Cook the fish for 3–4 minutes on each side, or until cooked through.

Meanwhile, combine the olives, lemon zest, parsley and olive oil in a bowl. Season with salt and pepper.

Transfer the fish to a serving platter and spoon the olive dressing over the top.

Serves 2

2 whole flounder (about 450 g each), cleaned (get your fish monger to do this)
15 green Sicilian olives, pitted and halved
1 tablespoon finely chopped preserved lemon zest
2 tablespoons chopped flat-leaf parsley
2 tablespoons olive oil
sea salt and freshly ground black pepper

Marinade
1 large handful each of flat-leaf parsley and coriander leaves (about 15 g each)
2 garlic cloves, chopped
2 tablespoons apple cider vinegar
1 long red or green chilli, deseeded and chopped
1 tablespoon smoked paprika
pinch of saffron threads
125 ml (½ cup) coconut oil, melted
sea salt and freshly ground black pepper

This recipe is inspired by my dear friend Jimmy Shu from the famous Hanuman restaurants in Darwin, Alice Springs and Adelaide. Jimmy, one of the nicest fellas in the industry, always blows me away with his food. One dish I often order is his barramundi meen moolie, which is gently poached in a delicious blend of coconut, turmeric and curry leaves. I have used mussels here but you can easily use chicken, fish or other seafood and add whatever vegetables you love. Try making this dish when you have a large group of people coming over. It's also a great way to get kids to try mussels — my daughters love the light curry-like sauce.

MUSSEL MOOLIE

1½ tablespoons coconut oil
1 onion, finely chopped
2 garlic cloves, finely chopped
½–1 small green chilli, deseeded and finely sliced (optional)
2 teaspoons finely grated ginger
2 teaspoons ground turmeric
15 fresh curry leaves (see note)
2 cinnamon sticks
6 cardamom pods
2 bay leaves
3 cloves
375 ml (1½ cups) coconut cream
1 kg mussels, scrubbed and debearded
12 cherry tomatoes, halved
sea salt and freshly ground black pepper
juice of ½ lemon
coriander leaves, to serve

Note

Curry leaves come from the curry tree, which is native to India and Sri Lanka. They are available both fresh and dried from Asian grocers and some supermarkets. Fresh curry leaves freeze really well if sealed in a zip-lock bag.

Heat the coconut oil in a wok or large saucepan over medium–high heat. Add the onion and cook for 5 minutes until softened. Stir in the garlic, chilli and ginger and cook for 30 seconds. Add the turmeric, curry leaves, cinnamon, cardamom, bay leaves and cloves and cook for a further 30 seconds until fragrant.

Pour the coconut cream into the pan, stir and bring to the boil. Add the mussels and cherry tomatoes, cover with a lid and cook for 5–6 minutes until the mussels open. Season with salt and pepper.

Stir through lemon juice serve garnished with the coriander leaves.

Serves 2

Taj Burrow is a very dear friend of mine, and is one of Australia's top surfing athletes and heroes. He is the kind of fella who likes to fuel his body well. Recently I was lucky enough to film him with his trainer and fellow paleo enthusiast Johnny Gannon. I asked the boys to have a surf with me and cook up one of the dishes they love to eat. They prepared this, their paleo version of fish and chips. Give this dish a shot for your next Friday fish night. I promise you will not be disappointed.

TAJ AND JOHNNY'S FISH AND CHIPS

2 large sweet potatoes (about 400 g each), sliced into 8 mm thick rounds
3½ tablespoons coconut oil, melted
sea salt
4 firm white fish fillets (such as snapper, barramundi, cod, sea bass, coral trout) (about 180 g each), skin left on
freshly ground black pepper
lemon wedges, to serve
1 handful of flat-leaf parsley leaves, roughly chopped (optional)

Salad
1 small handful of mixed sprouts
1 small handful of alfalfa sprouts
2 large handfuls of mixed salad leaves
1 avocado, sliced

Dressing
1 tablespoon finely grated ginger
1 garlic clove, finely chopped
3½ tablespoons extra-virgin olive oil
2½ tablespoons lemon juice
1½ tablespoons hulled hemp seeds*
sea salt and freshly ground black pepper

* See Glossary

Preheat the oven to 200°C. Lightly grease a large baking tray with a little coconut oil.

Spread the sweet potato on the prepared tray in a single layer and rub with 2 tablespoons of the coconut oil. Season with salt and bake for 10 minutes. Turn the sweet potato chips over and bake for a further 5 minutes until tender and lightly browned. (Keep a close eye on them as they can easily burn.)

Season the fish with salt and pepper and rub both sides with the remaining coconut oil. Heat a large non-stick frying pan over medium–high heat, then add the fish, skin-side up, and cook for 3 minutes until golden brown. Flip the fillets with a spatula and cook for a further 5 minutes until the skin is crispy and the fish cooked through.

Meanwhile, mix all of the dressing ingredients in a small bowl. Combine the sprouts, salad leaves and avocado in a large bowl. Pour over half of the dressing and gently toss.

Serve the fish and chips with the salad, lemon wedges and the remaining dressing on the side. Sprinkle some parsley over the fish, if desired.

Serves 4

If you have a fridge full of staples, a pantry full of spices and some herbs growing in the garden, you have the basics for creating quick, memorable dishes at any time. All you need to do is team these basics with the freshest raw ingredients. This recipe is exactly what I love about sensational quick cooking, as it takes some wild-caught fish and cooks it with a couple of fridge staples, in this case: caper berries and olives. I have used fresh tomatoes but you could also use canned whole peeled tomatoes or tomato passata. I love to serve this with a salad in summer or some simple veggies in winter.

PREP:
10 mins
COOK:
20 mins

FISH WITH TOMATO, OLIVES AND CAPER BERRIES

Heat the oil or fat in a large non-stick frying pan over medium heat. Add the shallot and cook for 2 minutes until translucent. Add the garlic, olives, caper berries and celery and cook for 4 minutes. Pour in the wine and simmer for 3 minutes, then stir in the tomato and half of the parsley. Simmer for 5 minutes until the tomato has broken down slightly.

Season the fish with some salt and pepper, then add to the pan in a single layer. Reduce the heat to low, cover with a lid and gently simmer for 4–5 minutes until the fish is cooked through. Carefully transfer the fish to serving plates and keep warm.

Season the sauce with some salt and pepper and stir in the olive oil. Pour the sauce over the fish, sprinkle over the remaining parsley and serve.

Serves 2

3 tablespoons coconut oil or other good-quality fat*
1 French shallot, chopped
3 garlic cloves, finely chopped
80 g (½ cup) pitted kalamata olives
8 caper berries*
½ small celery stalk, finely chopped
3 tablespoons white wine
3 Roma tomatoes, chopped
1 small handful of flat-leaf parsley, roughly chopped
4 fish fillets (about 300 g in total), skin on or off (red mullet, whiting or John Dory would all work well)
sea salt and freshly ground black pepper
1 tablespoon extra-virgin olive oil

See Glossary

Yum, yum, yum is all I can say. Fish has never tasted so good! A super-simple yet super-impressive recipe to get the tastebuds going, this dish will impress even the fussiest of eaters. Of course, you can play around with the protein and use chicken or prawns instead. Serve with some fermented veggies like kimchi on the side along with a salad or a bowl of steamed veggies.

QUICK FISH CURRY WITH ROASTED CAULIFLOWER

2 teaspoons ground turmeric
2 teaspoons ground coriander
½ head of cauliflower (about 450 g), broken into florets
4 tablespoons coconut oil, melted
pinch of sea salt
4 white fish fillets (about 180 g each), skin left on and pin-boned
juice of 2 limes
1 onion, sliced
2.5 cm piece of ginger, finely grated
4 garlic cloves, finely chopped
5 cardamom pods
1 cinnamon stick
1 teaspoon chilli flakes
pinch of freshly ground black pepper
12 fresh curry leaves (see note)
8 okra, halved
1 × 400 ml can coconut milk
140 ml fish stock or water
1 large handful of baby spinach leaves
1 tablespoon fish sauce
1 handful of coriander leaves, to serve (optional)

Note
Curry leaves come from the curry tree, which is native to India and Sri Lanka. They are available both fresh and dried from Asian grocers and some supermarkets. Fresh curry leaves freeze really well if sealed in a zip-lock bag.

Preheat the oven to 200°C. Lightly grease a baking tray with a little coconut oil.

Mix the ground spices together in a small bowl and set aside.

Place the cauliflower florets, 1 tablespoon of coconut oil and half of the spice mix in a large bowl and toss to combine. Transfer the spiced cauliflower to the prepared tray and spread out in a single layer. Season with salt and roast in the oven for 15 minutes until golden.

Meanwhile, rub the remaining spice mix into the flesh side of the fish fillets, then squeeze over the juice of 1 lime. Cover with plastic wrap and leave to marinate in the fridge for 10 minutes.

While the fish is marinating, heat the remaining coconut oil in a large frying pan over medium heat. Add the onion and sauté gently for 5 minutes until softened and translucent. Add the ginger, garlic, cardamom, cinnamon, chilli flakes, pepper and curry leaves and cook for a further 1 minute until fragrant. Stir in the roasted cauliflower, okra, coconut milk and fish stock or water, then add the fish, flesh-side down, and gently simmer for 8–10 minutes until the fish is nearly cooked through. Gently mix in the spinach leaves and cook until just wilted, about 30 seconds.

To finish, season with the fish sauce (adding more to taste if desired), squeeze over the remaining lime juice and garnish with coriander leaves (if using).

Serves 4

TIP

Any firm white fish, such as snapper, cod, sea bass or bream, will work well in this recipe.

I love that we use the word 'spice' when we talk about adding variety and excitement to our lives. For me, spices are the key to good cooking. They are so versatile and can transform bland and boring ingredients into a truly memorable meal. When used well, spices are capable of creating harmonious balancing acts on our palates that range from faint and subtle to heady and complex. I urge you to expand your spice collection and research the benefits of spices and herbs. Serve this dish with cooked vegetables or a fresh salad.

JAMAICAN MUSSEL AND CLAM CURRY

2 tablespoons coconut oil
1 onion, finely chopped
3 garlic cloves, finely chopped
3 cm piece of ginger, finely chopped
2 teaspoons curry powder
1 teaspoon ground turmeric
1 teaspoon ground allspice
2 tomatoes, deseeded and roughly chopped
1 long red chilli, deseeded and finely chopped
1 teaspoon thyme leaves, chopped
sea salt and freshly ground black pepper
500 ml (2 cups) coconut cream
1 kg mussels, scrubbed and debearded
15 clams, cleaned
1 handful of coriander leaves, chopped

Heat the coconut oil in a wok or very large saucepan over medium heat. Add the onion and cook, stirring occasionally, until softened, about 5 minutes. Add the garlic and ginger and cook, stirring, for 1 minute. Add the curry powder, turmeric and allspice and cook, continuing to stir, for 1 minute. Add the tomato, chilli and thyme and cook for 2 minutes until the tomato begins to break down. Season with salt and pepper.

Pour the coconut cream into the pan and bring to the boil. Reduce the heat to medium–low and simmer for 10 minutes to allow the flavours to develop.

Add the mussels and clams to the curry, cover with a lid, gently give the pan a shake, then cook for 4–6 minutes until the mussels and clams open. Stir in the coriander and serve.

Serves 2

People often ask me the secret to good cooking. My answer is to start with the best ingredients you can afford and to use fresh herbs and spices, but the real key to making food taste great is to work with the classics. Every good chef knows and respects this. This recipe combines humble ingredients in an unforgettable way.

PREP:
10 mins
COOK:
15 mins

SNAPPER ACQUA PAZZA (FISH IN CRAZY WATER)

Make three cuts down to the bone on each side of the fish.

Heat 1 tablespoon of the oil or fat in a large frying pan over medium–high heat. Add one of the fish and cook for 3–4 minutes until lightly golden. Turn the fish and add half each of the garlic, chilli, cherry tomatoes and olives to the pan and season with some salt and pepper. After 30 seconds, pour in half of the mineral water and scatter on half of the basil and cook for another couple of minutes until the fish is just done. Transfer to a large plate and keep warm while you repeat this process with the remaining ingredients. Serve with the lemon wedges.

Serves 2

2 whole snapper or other firm white fish (about 800 g in total), cleaned and scaled
2 tablespoons coconut oil or other good-quality fat*
10 garlic cloves, roasted and peeled
1 long red chilli, deseeded and finely sliced
250 g cherry tomatoes, halved
25 Ligurian olives (see note)
sea salt and freshly ground black pepper
300 ml sparkling mineral water
1 large handful of basil leaves
lemon wedges, to serve

See Glossary

Note

Small and quite sweet, Ligurian olives are picked as they are turning from green to black. They are available from gourmet food stores and delicatessens. If you can't find them, use any other variety of olive that you love.

Entertaining in a flash

Make a loaf of delicious and nourishing **PALEO BREAD** (page 257) or seed and nut bread (page 256) as well as some cashew cheese (page 256) on the weekend so that you have them on hand to serve with some olives when friends pop round.

Prawns are perfect for entertaining as they are so quick and can be served either warm or cold. For a really speedy prawn dish, peel some cooked king prawns and toss with extra-virgin olive oil, chopped dill, lemon juice, salt and pepper. Arrange the prawns on a platter and serve.

My wife Nic loves whipping up a batch of **kale chips** when friends pop around. Place some sunflower seeds, sun-dried tomatoes, garlic, lemon juice, coconut oil and sea salt in a food processor and blend to a coarse paste. Transfer the paste to a large bowl and add some chopped kale, then toss to coat evenly. Arrange the kale in a single layer on a lined baking tray and bake in a 180°C oven for 10–15 minutes, or until crispy. Cool before serving.

Ceviche is one of my go-to dishes when I'm looking for something fast yet impressive to serve for friends on a weeknight. Try my Asian ceviche salad (page 92) or ceviche with pomegranate and mango (page 102).

To make a quick and easy pâté, heat 1 tablespoon of coconut oil in a saucepan over medium heat. Add 500 g of chicken livers, 2 crushed garlic cloves and 125 ml of bone broth or water. Simmer for 3–5 minutes, or until the livers are almost cooked through. Transfer the liver, garlic and any remaining liquid to a food processor and blend on high until smooth and thick. Season to taste. Cool completely before serving with some paleo bread (page 257) or fresh vegetable sticks.

GAZPACHO is great for entertaining as you can make it the day before. Place some really ripe tomatoes, red onion, garlic, capsicum and cucumber in a food processor and blend until smooth. Add a little sherry vinegar, season to taste and refrigerate overnight. When ready to serve, spoon the gazpacho into bowls and add some picked crab meat or cooked peeled prawns to each bowl. Gazpacho can also be frozen for up to 2 months and then thawed a couple of hours before your guests arrive.

PREP:
7 mins
(+ 12–24 hrs to marinate)
cook:
20 mins

This recipe is special to me as I made it with my friend Tony Coote for the first TV series of *The Paleo Way*. Tony, a biodynamic farmer who owns Mulloon Creek Natural Farms, isn't that confident in the kitchen — and I loved that because it meant I could show him how to create amazing flavoured dishes in a short amount of time and with little fuss. I decided we would cook up a roast chook with Indian spices. The result was stunning. Here I have simplified the dish and sped up the cooking process by using chicken drumsticks, but you could use marylands or wings. Serve with a salad or veggies and some fermented veg, too.

INDIAN-STYLE ROAST CHICKEN DRUMSTICKS

1.2 kg chicken drumsticks
2 tablespoons coconut oil or
   other good-quality fat*, melted
sea salt and freshly ground
   black pepper
1 large handful of coriander
   leaves, roughly chopped
juice of 2 lemons

Indian spice marinade
2 teaspoons coriander seeds
2 teaspoons cumin seeds
1 teaspoon sea salt
3 teaspoons ground turmeric
2½ teaspoons garam masala
¼ teaspoon chilli powder (add
   more if you like it spicy)
3 garlic cloves, finely chopped
2 tablespoons finely grated
   ginger

* See Glossary

To make the Indian spice marinade, combine the coriander and cumin seeds in a dry frying pan and toast over medium heat until fragrant, 1–2 minutes. Remove from the heat and allow to cool. Grind the spices in a spice grinder or mortar and pestle. Mix the ground spices with the remaining marinade ingredients in a large bowl.

Add the chicken to the spice mix and massage until evenly coated. Cover the bowl with plastic wrap and refrigerate overnight. For best results, marinate for 24 hours so the flavours develop fully.

Preheat the oven to 180°C.

Brush the spiced drumsticks with the oil or fat and arrange in a roasting tin in a single layer. Add 4 tablespoons of water. Roast for 20 minutes, turning halfway through cooking, until the chicken is cooked through and golden. Taste and season with salt and pepper, if needed.

Place the chicken on a large platter, then pour over the juices from the tin. Sprinkle with the coriander leaves and squeeze over the lemon juice.

Serves 4

I have no doubt this recipe will become a favourite. I have taken the classic schnitzel and, to make it anti-inflammatory, reinvented it without using any grain- or dairy-based products. You could swap the chicken for chicken livers or hearts, some wild-caught seafood, or pretty much any other animal protein. Serve with a large salad or cooked vegetables and, of course, some fermented veggies on the side. You can even wrap the chicken up in lettuce or cabbage leaves and slather it with a flavoured mayonnaise or aioli.

PISTACHIO-CRUSTED CHICKEN WITH SPICY AIOLI

800 g chicken breast fillets, cut lengthways into 2.5 cm strips and patted dry with paper towel
150 g (1 cup) pistachio nuts
100 g (1 cup) almond meal
2 tablespoons finely chopped flat-leaf parsley leaves
1½ teaspoons chilli flakes (optional)
1 teaspoon garlic powder
1 teaspoon onion powder
sea salt and freshly ground black pepper
2 eggs
2 tablespoons coconut cream or almond milk
100 g (⅔ cup) tapioca flour*
coconut oil or other good-quality fat*, for frying
lemon halves, to serve

Spicy aioli
150 g Aioli (page 242)
½ teaspoon harissa paste, or to taste
½ teaspoon finely chopped preserved lemon zest

* See Glossary

To make the spicy aioli, mix together the aioli, harissa and preserved lemon. Set aside until needed.

Blitz the pistachios to a fine crumb in a food processor. Transfer to a shallow bowl, add the almond meal, parsley, chilli flakes (if using), garlic powder, onion powder, a pinch each of salt and pepper and mix well.

Place the eggs and coconut cream or almond milk in a shallow bowl and whisk well. Place the tapioca flour in another shallow bowl.

One by one dust the chicken strips in the tapioca flour, shake off any excess flour, dip in the egg mixture and then coat in the nut crumb mixture, making sure you cover the entire chicken strip thoroughly. If there are areas that are not entirely coated, simply dab a little more egg mixture onto the dry spot and coat again with the nut crumbs.

Heat the oil or fat in a large frying pan over medium–high heat. Add the crumbed chicken strips, in batches, and cook for 2½–3 minutes on each side until golden brown and cooked through. Drain on paper towel. Allow to cool slightly before serving. Season with salt, if needed.

Serve the pistachio-crusted chicken with the spicy aioli and some lemon cheeks on the side.

Serves 4

Yakitori is the name given to the classic Japanese street food of chicken skewers grilled over charcoal and served with salt or a simple sauce. The meat can be marinated in the sauce to enhance the flavours and different meats can be used. I love to use chicken livers, hearts and skin-on thigh fillets and thread them separately onto skewers, as each has a different cooking time – it is ideal to have the livers still pink in the middle, whereas you want to cook the thigh fillets all the way through. Also try adding some different veggies to the skewers – mushrooms, onions and okra are favourites.

PREP:
10 mins
(+ 1 hr to marinate)
COOK:
13 mins

YAKITORI CHICKEN SKEWERS

To make the marinade, place the ingredients in a large bowl and whisk until combined. Pour over the chicken, toss well and set aside to marinate for at least 1 hour, or overnight in the fridge.

Thread alternating pieces of the chicken, shiitake mushrooms and spring onion onto eight skewers.

Heat a barbecue plate or chargrill pan to hot. Grill the skewers, basting with the marinade and turning often, for 6–8 minutes until the chicken is browned and cooked through.

Place the remaining marinade in a saucepan, bring to the boil and simmer for 2–5 minutes until thickened slightly. Remove from the heat and transfer to a small serving bowl.

To make the dressing, combine all the ingredients in a bowl and whisk well.

To make the salad, place all the ingredients in a bowl, then pour on some of the dressing and toss gently. Season with an extra pinch of salt and pepper, if desired.

Place the skewers on serving plates, drizzle on some more dressing, sprinkle on the sesame seeds and garnish with the shiso leaves. Serve with the salad on the side.

Serves 4

600 g chicken thigh fillets, cut into 2.5 cm cubes
16 fresh shiitake mushrooms, halved
6 spring onions, chopped into 4 cm lengths
toasted sesame seeds, to serve
baby shiso leaves*, to serve

Marinade
6 tablespoons tamari or coconut aminos*
4 tablespoons honey
2 garlic cloves, finely chopped
1 tablespoon finely grated ginger

Dressing
3 tablespoons tamari or coconut aminos*
2 tablespoons apple cider vinegar
pinch each of sea salt and freshly ground black pepper
½ teaspoon mustard powder
1 tablespoon macadamia oil or olive oil
2 teaspoons sesame oil

Salad
1 small carrot, finely sliced lengthways into ribbons
1 cucumber, finely sliced lengthways into ribbons
5 cm piece of daikon*, finely sliced lengthways into ribbons
2 red radishes, finely sliced
1 spring onion, finely sliced

* See Glossary

TIP

Use a mandoline to finely slice all of the vegetables for the salad – it will save time and ensure that all of the veggies are super thin.

PREP:
20 mins
COOK:
22 mins
(+ 5 mins to rest)

Michelle Tam, author of the food blog and cookbook Nom Nom Paleo, is loved by millions around the world for her no-nonsense approach to cooking paleo food. Mich prepared this recipe for me at her home in San Francisco while I was filming the first series of *The Paleo Way* for TV. I love the simplicity of this cooking technique and I also love to cook duck breast this way so it gets really crispy skin. Serve with a generous salad or cooked green vegetables and some fermented veg for good measure.

CRACKLING CHICKEN

8 chicken thigh fillets, skin left on
1 tablespoon sea salt
2 teaspoons coconut oil or other good-quality fat*
2 teaspoons spice mix of your choice (I like using a Cajun or Moroccan mix)
lemon wedges, to serve

See Glossary

Flatten the chicken thighs with a mallet to ensure they cook evenly. Season the skin with salt.

Melt the oil or fat in a large, heavy-based frying pan over medium–high heat. Place four of the chicken thighs, skin-side down, in the hot pan and season the exposed side with 1 teaspoon of the seasoning. If your seasoning doesn't include salt, you may wish to add a little.

Fry the chicken, undisturbed, for 6–8 minutes until crispy and golden brown. Flip the chicken over and cook for 3 minutes, or until cooked through. Remove from the pan and keep warm. Repeat with the remaining chicken.

Serve with the lemon wedges and your favourite vegetables or salad.

Serves 4

Tip

If you are using duck, make sure you cook it over very low heat to allow the fat to render and give you the most amazingly crispy skin.

Mmmmm, carbonara is a dish that I used to cook for staff meals in my apprenticeship days 25 years ago. Back then we basically lived off low-cost pasta and rice dishes and I have to confess that I absolutely loved them — though I usually felt horrible an hour or two later. As this whole paleo thing is not about restriction but more about celebration, I have reinvented the classic carbonara, and it tastes just as good, if not better, than the original. Play around with different vegetables. Parsnip and pumpkin are favourites and make great noodles when put through a spiraliser, or try spaghetti squash or kelp noodles, if you prefer.

ZUCCHINI CARBONARA

2 tablespoons duck fat or
   coconut oil
6 rashers of rindless bacon
   (about 350 g), diced
2 onions, finely chopped
4 garlic cloves, finely chopped
3 tablespoons finely chopped
   flat-leaf parsley
600 g zucchini, ends trimmed, cut
   into long thin spaghetti strips
   with a vegetable spiraliser
sea salt and freshly ground
   black pepper
4 egg yolks
truffle-infused olive oil (optional)
finely grated macadamia nuts,
   to serve
pinch of chilli flakes, to serve
   (optional)

Egg sauce
2 eggs
1 tablespoon tapioca flour*
375 ml (1½ cups) chicken or
   vegetable stock, or water
125 ml (½ cup) coconut cream
sea salt and freshly ground
   black pepper

See Glossary

To make the egg sauce, whisk together the eggs and tapioca flour in a small bowl. Set aside. Place the stock and coconut cream in a small saucepan and bring to the boil. Add half of the hot liquid to the egg and tapioca flour mixture and whisk to combine, then whisk in the remaining hot liquid. Return the mixture to the pan and place over low heat. Cook, stirring constantly with a wooden spoon or whisk, for 5 minutes, or until the sauce thickens. Season with salt and pepper and set aside, keeping warm.

Heat the fat or oil in a large frying pan over medium–high heat. Add the bacon and cook for 2–3 minutes, or until it just starts to colour. Reduce the heat to medium, then add the onion and garlic and cook for 8 minutes until translucent and softened. Stir in the parsley and zucchini and cook for 2 minutes until softened. Remove from the heat, pour over the egg sauce and toss gently. Season to taste.

Divide the carbonara between serving plates and place an egg yolk on top of each. Drizzle on the truffle oil (if using), sprinkle over some grated macadamias and black pepper or chilli flakes, if desired, and serve.

Serves 4

TIP

A veggie spiraliser is an essential tool in the kitchen if you want to make delicious vegetable noodles. See page 13 for more information.

I have shared a recipe for a paleo pizza base before, but this one is even healthier as it contains cauliflower. It involves a little more work than a traditional flour, water and yeast base, but the good news is that it takes less time to get it on the table, as you don't need to wait for the dough to rise. Top it with whatever toppings you love. I have kept it simple and delicious by using a tomato and basil base with prosciutto and rocket. Serve with a fresh salad.

PREP:
20 mins
(+ 10 mins to cool)
COOK:
15 mins

PROSCIUTTO PIZZA

Preheat the oven to 180°C. Grease a baking tray with oil and line with baking paper. Lightly grease another sheet of baking paper with oil.

To make the pizza sauce, place all the ingredients in a blender and puree until smooth. Set aside.

To make the cauliflower pizza base, place the cauliflower in a food processor bowl and pulse to a rice consistency. Heat 1 tablespoon of the coconut oil in a frying pan over medium heat. Cook the cauliflower rice for 4–6 minutes, or until soft. Allow to cool for 5–10 minutes. Transfer the cauliflower to a clean tea towel, gather in the edges and twist out the excess liquid. Place the cauliflower, almond meal, egg, remaining coconut oil and salt and pepper in a bowl and mix well to form a batter.

Mound the cauliflower batter on the centre of the lined tray, then place the sheet of greased baking paper on top. Using a palette knife or your hands, spread out evenly to form a 30 cm round. Carefully remove the top layer of paper and set aside. Bake for 10 minutes until cooked through. Remove and cool slightly.

Gently flip the cauliflower base onto the reserved baking paper and peel away the top layer of paper. Return the cauliflower base to the baking tray and evenly spread with 4 tablespoons of pizza sauce. Scatter on the basil and tomato and season with salt and pepper. Bake for 5 minutes until the crust is lightly golden and crispy.

Meanwhile, dress the rocket with the balsamic vinegar and olive oil and toss until the leaves are well coated. Season with salt, if desired.

Slide the pizza onto a chopping board and scatter over the rocket leaves, prosciutto and pear. Slice and serve.

Serves 2

8 basil leaves, torn
1 Roma tomato, finely sliced
1 large handful of rocket leaves
1 teaspoon balsamic vinegar
1 tablespoon extra-virgin olive oil
pinch of sea salt (optional)
6 slices of prosciutto
½ pear, finely sliced

Pizza sauce
200 g canned whole peeled
    tomatoes
pinch each of sea salt and freshly
    ground black pepper
½ teaspoon dried oregano

Cauliflower pizza base
340 g cauliflower, chopped
    into florets
1½ tablespoons coconut oil
60 g almond meal
1 egg
½ teaspoon sea salt
2 pinches of freshly ground
    white pepper

* See Glossary

Tip
- - - - - - - - - - - - - - - - - - -
Leftover pizza sauce can be stored in an airtight container in the fridge for up to 3 days

One thing is certain, if food is crumbed and fried it is delicious. This mouth-watering recipe is inspired by the Japanese classic katsu – a crispy coated meat dish with a unique curry sauce. I know it will become a firm favourite of yours. I have chosen to use pork, but you could easily make this with chicken, fish, prawns, beef, lamb or goat. It goes very well with this simple cabbage salad.

PORK KATSU WITH CURRY SAUCE

4 pork loins (about 180 g each)
250 g (2½ cups) almond meal
  or macadamia meal
1 teaspoon onion powder
1 teaspoon garlic powder
½ teaspoon chilli powder
80 g (heaped ½ cup) tapioca flour*
2 eggs
4 tablespoons coconut milk
coconut oil, for shallow frying
Cauliflower Rice, to serve
  (page 208)
baby shiso leaves*, to serve
½ teaspoon chilli flakes

Curry sauce
1 tablespoon coconut oil or other
  good-quality fat*
1 small onion, finely chopped
3 garlic cloves, finely chopped
2 carrots, chopped
2 tablespoons tapioca flour*
1½ tablespoons good-quality
  curry powder
600 ml chicken stock or water,
  plus extra if needed
1 tablespoon honey (optional)
1 tablespoon tamari or coconut
  aminos*

1 bay leaf
½ teaspoon garam masala
sea salt and freshly ground
  black pepper

Cabbage salad
¼ Savoy cabbage, shredded
2 red radishes, julienned
2 tablespoons apple cider vinegar
80 ml (⅓ cup) extra-virgin
  olive oil
1 spring onion, finely sliced
2 teaspoon toasted sesame seeds

See Glossary

To make the curry sauce, heat the oil or fat in a saucepan over medium heat. Add the onion, garlic and carrot and cook for 8 minutes until the carrot is tender. Stir in the tapioca flour and curry powder and cook for 30 seconds. Slowly pour in the stock, a little at a time, mixing to prevent lumps, then stir in the honey (if using), tamari or coconut aminos, bay leaf and garam masala and bring to the boil. Reduce the heat and simmer for 20 minutes, or until the vegetables are very tender and the sauce is thick. Puree the sauce with a hand-held blender, season with salt and pepper and thin with extra stock or water if necessary.

While the curry sauce is cooking, place the pork loins between two sheets of baking paper and pound with a meat mallet until about 1 cm thick. Combine the nut meal and spice powders in a shallow bowl with a little salt and pepper and mix well. Place the tapioca flour in another shallow bowl. In a third bowl, whisk the eggs and coconut milk until combined. Working with one piece at a time, dust the pounded pork with the tapioca flour, shaking off any excess, then dip in the egg mixture and evenly coat in the nut meal.

Heat the oil in a large deep frying pan over medium–high heat until it reaches about 160°C. (To test, place a tiny piece of pork in the hot oil – if it immediately starts to bubble around the pork, the oil is ready.) Fry the pork for 3–5 minutes on each side until golden and cooked through. Remove from the pan and drain on paper towel. Season with salt and pepper.

To make the salad, toss all the ingredients into a bowl and season with a little salt and pepper.

Place the pork on serving plates, pour over some curry sauce and serve with the cauliflower rice, cabbage salad and baby shiso. Finish with a sprinkle of chilli flakes.

Serves 4

What I love about the paleo movement is seeing the resurgence in pasture-raised and free-range pork, and I look forward to the day when the inhumane practice of factory farming is a distant memory. This super-simple preparation will have the whole family smiling from ear to ear. Make sure you serve the skewers with some fermented veg and a lovely green salad.

SATAY PORK SKEWERS

800 g pork loin, cut into
    2.5 cm cubes
sea salt and freshly ground
    black pepper
coriander leaves, to serve
lime wedges, to serve

Marinade
1½ teaspoons lime zest
1½ tablespoons lime juice
1 tablespoon coconut oil, melted,
    plus extra for cooking
2 tablespoons tamari
1½ tablespoons fish sauce
3 garlic cloves, crushed
1½ tablespoons finely grated
    ginger
1½ tablespoons ground turmeric
1½ teaspoons ground coriander
1 teaspoon ground cumin
pinch sea salt

Macadamia satay sauce
155 g (1 cup) macadamia nuts
120 g (½ cup) almond butter
2 tablespoons finely grated
    ginger
1 long red chilli, deseeded and
    finely chopped
2 tablespoons tamari or coconut
    aminos*
1 tablespoon sesame oil
1 tablespoon maple syrup
    (optional)
sea salt

See Glossary

Combine the marinade ingredients in a large bowl and mix well. Add the pork and toss until thoroughly coated. Cover with plastic wrap and place in the fridge to marinate for at least 2 hours, or overnight.

Soak eight bamboo skewers in a shallow dish of cold water for 20 minutes. Drain.

Meanwhile, to make the macadamia satay sauce, combine the macadamia nuts and almond butter in a food processor bowl and pulse until well ground. Add the ginger and chilli and process until blended. Pour in the tamari or coconut aminos, sesame oil and maple syrup (if using) and blend well. Gradually pour in 120 ml of water and pulse until the sauce is smooth. If the sauce is a little too thick, simply add more water. Season with a little salt, if desired.

Heat a barbecue plate or chargrill pan to medium–hot. Thread the marinated pork cubes onto the prepared skewers and season with salt and pepper. Cook the skewers, basting with the marinade, for 3 minutes on each side until browned and cooked through. Scatter the coriander leaves over the skewers and serve with the lime wedges and the satay sauce on the side.

Serves 4

One of my intentions with this book was to take classics from around the world that my family and I love to eat and show you how we have made them paleo so we can still enjoy them. This classic Turkish dish is a delicious concoction of spiced meat and greens encased in pastry. Here we have simply created a paleo pastry to wrap around the mince, and it certainly doesn't lack any of the flavour or texture of the original version. Delectable served with some fermented veggies on the side.

PREP:
12 mins
(+ 5 mins to cool)
COOK:
20 mins

GOZLEME OF LAMB, MINT AND SPINACH

Preheat the oven to 180°C and line a large baking tray with baking paper.

To make the gozleme base, combine the almond meal, tapioca flour or tapioca flour and salt in a large bowl. In a separate bowl, whisk together the eggs, oil, coconut yoghurt and 1 tablespoon of water. Fold the egg mixture into the dry ingredients, one-third at a time, and mix thoroughly to form a smooth, thick batter.

Spoon the batter onto the prepared tray and, using a palette knife or spatula, spread out to form a 1 mm thick rectangular shape about 36 cm × 26 cm. Bake for 5–7 minutes until cooked through.

To make the mint yoghurt, combine all the ingredients in a small bowl.

Meanwhile, melt half of the oil in a frying pan over medium heat. Add the lamb and cook, stirring to break up any lumps, for 5 minutes until browned. Reduce the heat to medium–low and add the garlic, cumin, chilli flakes and passata. Season with salt and pepper. Cook for another minute, or until dry.

Spread the spinach or silverbeet over half of the gozleme base, then add the lamb and mint and season. Fold the base with the baking paper over to enclose the filling and press down lightly.

Heat a barbecue plate or chargrill pan to hot. Brush one side of the gozleme with a little of the remaining coconut oil and cook until golden, about 3 minutes. Brush the top with the remaining coconut oil, turn and cook until golden. Cut into four pieces and serve with the lemon wedges and mint yoghurt on the side.

Serves 4

2 tablespoons coconut oil
200 g lamb mince
1 garlic clove, finely chopped
¼ teaspoon ground cumin
pinch of chilli flakes
3 tablespoons tomato passata
freshly ground black pepper
50 g baby spinach or silverbeet leaves
4 mint leaves, chopped
lemon wedges, to serve

Gozleme base

130 g (scant 1⅓ cups) almond meal
65 g (scant ½ cup) tapioca flour*
½ teaspoon sea salt
2 eggs
3 tablespoons macadamia oil or melted coconut oil
3 tablespoons coconut yoghurt

Mint yoghurt

3 tablespoons coconut yoghurt
1 tablespoon water
4 mint leaves, finely sliced
pinch of sumac*

See Glossary

I love spicy food that makes my tastebuds come alive and Portuguese piri-piri is one of my favourites. Well balanced and full of flavour, in my book, piri-piri is the perfect accompaniment to any type of meat, especially chicken. Here I have teamed it with chicken livers as I adore them in any form; however, if you are not a fan, simply replace them with chicken thigh fillets with the skin on. I encourage you to eat this with one of the vegetable dishes in this book or another of your favourites that you love to cook.

PIRI-PIRI CHICKEN SKEWERS

800 g chicken livers, sinew removed
2 tablespoons coconut oil or other good-quality fat*
coriander leaves, to serve
4 lemon wedges, to serve

Piri-piri sauce
2 tablespoons coconut oil or other good-quality fat*
2 tablespoons sweet paprika
1 tablespoon ground cumin
1 tablespoon ground coriander
1 red capsicum, chopped
½ onion, chopped
2 long red chillies, deseeded and roughly chopped
1 teaspoon finely grated ginger
juice of 1 lemon
170 ml (⅔ cup) coconut oil, melted
sea salt and freshly ground black pepper

* See Glossary

To make the piri-piri sauce, combine 1 tablespoon of the oil or fat, the paprika, cumin and coriander in a frying pan over medium heat and cook until fragrant, about 30 seconds. Add the remaining coconut oil, then the capsicum, onion, chilli and ginger and cook for 3 minutes until soft and translucent. Stir in the lemon juice, then transfer the mixture to a blender and blend until smooth. Pour in the melted coconut oil and blend until incorporated. Season with salt and pepper. Allow to cool for 5 minutes.

Place the chicken livers in a bowl and add half of the piri-piri sauce. Mix thoroughly, cover with plastic wrap and marinate in the fridge for 1 hour. Soak eight bamboo skewers in water for 20 minutes.

Thread the livers onto the prepared skewers, about four per skewer. Drizzle a little oil or fat over the livers.

Heat a barbecue plate or chargrill pan to hot. Cook the skewers for 2 minutes on each side, or until cooked to your liking, basting with the extra marinade from the bowl. Remove from the pan, sprinkle over some coriander and serve with the lemon wedges and a simple garden salad.

Serves 4

TIP

If you are not keen on chicken livers, you could use chicken thigh fillets instead. You will need to cook them for longer though – about 3–4 minutes on each side, or until cooked through.

Whenever I speak to people about adopting a paleo lifestyle, I encourage them to start off with budget-friendly meals that the whole family is used to eating. Sausages are one of my favourite foods, and we usually have them once a week. I am fortunate to live near some passionate butchers who make paleo sausages the old-fashioned way, combining the best meat and fat from humanely raised animals with just the right amount of seasoning and spice. When buying snags, you need to become a bit of a detective — always read the label or ask what they are filled with. Oh and if you can find snags that include offal, then go for it!

FENNEL SAUSAGES WITH ONION GRAVY

600 ml beef stock
2 tablespoons coconut oil
 or other good-quality fat*
8 pork and fennel sausages
1 large onion, sliced
3 portobello mushrooms, sliced
2 tablespoons tapioca flour*
10 thyme sprigs, leaves picked
1½ tablespoons balsamic vinegar
1 tablespoon Worcestershire
 sauce
sea salt and freshly ground
 black pepper
chopped flat-leaf parsley,
 to serve

* See Glossary

Pour the beef stock into a saucepan, bring to the boil and cook for 6–8 minutes until reduced by half. Remove from the heat and set aside until needed.

Heat the oil or fat in a large frying pan over medium heat. Add the sausages and cook until browned on all sides and almost cooked through, about 8 minutes. Remove the sausages from the pan and set aside.

Add the onion to the same pan and cook over medium heat for 5 minutes until softened and starting to caramelise. Add the mushrooms and cook for 2 minutes until tender. Add the tapioca flour, stirring constantly for 1 minute, then add the thyme. Gradually pour in the stock, vinegar and Worcestershire sauce and mix well. Bring to the boil and simmer for 5 minutes until the sauce has thickened. Season with salt and pepper.

Return the sausages to the pan and cook for 2 minutes until they are completely cooked through. Sprinkle over the parsley and serve with a crisp salad.

Serves 4

The Japanese know how to respect ingredients and I gravitate towards their style of cooking because it is clean, intelligent and downright delicious. And, if you think about it, sashimi is probably the most primal of all dishes: raw sliced seafood or meat served with a little lemon juice or fermented soy and a touch of wasabi. Culinary heaven! I thought it only fitting that we pop this recipe in the book, as this simple preparation takes the humble steak to new levels. Serve this with a daikon and cucumber salad (page 179), some cooked broccoli and a side of fermented veg.

PREP:
15 mins
COOK:
5 mins
(+ 4 mins to rest)

JAPANESE BEEF TATAKI

To make the onion ponzu, place all the ingredients in a bowl, stir to combine and set aside.

To make the tataki dressing, place all the ingredients in a bowl and mix well. Set aside.

Heat a barbecue plate or chargrill pan to hot. Lightly brush the beef fillet with some coconut oil and season with salt and pepper. Sear the beef for 1½ minutes on all sides (or cook to your liking). Rest the beef in a warm place for 4 minutes.

Thinly slice the beef and arrange on a serving plate. Drizzle over the onion ponzu and tataki dressing, then top with the spring onion, bonito flakes, shiso, nori and sesame seeds.

Serves 4

600 g beef fillet, trimmed of fat and cut into 2 portions lengthways (bring the meat to room temperature before cooking)
melted coconut oil, for cooking
sea salt and freshly ground black pepper

Onion ponzu
½ onion, very finely chopped
1 garlic clove, very finely chopped
3 tablespoons olive oil or macadamia oil
1 tablespoon lemon juice
1 tablespoon apple cider vinegar
1 tablespoon tamari or coconut aminos*
½ teaspoon finely chopped ginger

Tataki dressing
2½ tablespoons tamari or coconut aminos*
125 ml (½ cup) apple cider vinegar
1 tablespoon bonito flakes*

To serve
2 spring onions, finely sliced
2 tablespoons bonito flakes*
baby shiso leaves*
1 nori sheet*, finely shredded
black sesame seeds

See Glossary

PREP:
1 min
(+ 5 mins for chimichurri
& 4 mins to rest)

COOK:
7 mins

All around the world in so many cuisines we see similar philosophies that promote the use of simple and honest ingredients – and nothing sums this up more than the classic and versatile chimichurri, an Argentinean recipe that is a beautiful balance of fresh and dried herbs, chilli, spices, vinegar or lemon juice and oil. Thailand has its own version, the classic nam jim, Vietnam has nuoc cham, Italy has salsa verde, France has gribiche and Spain has escabeche, just to name a few. I see chimichurri as one of the easiest ways to elevate a piece of gorgeous grass-fed steak or wild-caught fish or grilled mushroom.

BARBECUED STEAK WITH CHIMICHURRI

4 sirloin or scotch fillet steaks
  (about 200 g each)
3 tablespoons coconut oil
sea salt and freshly ground
  black pepper
100 g beef marrow (no bone),
  chopped
Chimichurri (page 251), to serve
lemon wedges, to serve

Remove the steaks from the fridge at least 15 minutes before cooking so they come to room temperature. Heat a barbecue plate or chargrill pan to hot.

Coat the steaks with a little coconut oil and season with salt and pepper. Cook the steaks for 2½–3 minutes, or until browned, then flip over and cook for another 2½–3 minutes for medium–rare. Transfer to a plate, cover with foil and rest in a warm place for 4 minutes.

Reduce the barbecue or pan to medium heat. Add the chopped marrow and cook for 1 minute until lightly golden and cooked through. Season with salt and pepper and then stir through the chimichurri.

Spoon some chimichurri and bone marrow over each steak and serve with a seasonal salad of your choice and a wedge of lemon.

Serves 4

Does any dish epitomise comfort food more than spaghetti and meatballs? Here I have used parsnip noodles in place of pasta, but you could use spaghetti squash, zucchini, pumpkin or sweet potato noodles, or even pop the meatballs on kelp noodles or a bed of broccoli or cauliflower rice. Play around with adding some liver, heart or kidneys to the meatball mix or perhaps some diced bacon. I love to serve this with a salad or vegetables and always include some fermented veggies on the side.

SPAGHETTI AND MEATBALLS

4 tablespoons coconut oil
1 French shallot, finely chopped
2 garlic cloves, finely chopped
2 handfuls of baby spinach leaves, chopped
350 g pork mince
150 g beef mince
80 g chicken livers, sinew removed, finely chopped
2 tablespoons finely chopped flat-leaf parsley leaves
1 egg yolk
sea salt and freshly ground black pepper

Tomato sauce
2 tablespoons coconut oil
2 garlic cloves, finely sliced
500 g canned crushed tomatoes
8 basil leaves

Spaghetti
6 parsnips (about 900 g in total), cut into spaghetti strips using a veggie spiraliser (see page 13)
2 tablespoons extra-virgin olive oil

To serve
chopped flat-leaf parsley or torn basil leaves
2 macadamia nuts, finely grated

To make the tomato sauce, melt the oil in a saucepan over medium heat. Add the garlic and fry for 1 minute until lightly browned. Stir in the tomatoes and 125 ml of water, then simmer for 10 minutes. Add the basil and simmer for a further 5 minutes. Season with salt and pepper and blend with a hand-held blender until smooth.

Meanwhile, melt 2 tablespoons of the coconut oil in a frying pan over medium heat. Add the shallot and garlic and fry for 3 minutes until the shallot is translucent and the garlic is lightly browned. Add the spinach and cook for a minute or so to wilt. Transfer to a bowl and set aside to cool.

Preheat the oven to 180°C.

In a large bowl, combine the pork and beef minces, chicken liver, spinach mixture, parsley, egg yolk and salt and pepper and mix well. Roll the mixture into golf ball–sized meatballs.

Melt the remaining coconut oil in an ovenproof frying pan over medium heat and fry the meatballs for 1½ minutes on one side. Turn the meatballs, then transfer the pan to the oven for 5 minutes until the meatballs are cooked through. Pour the tomato sauce into the pan, cover with a lid and keep warm on the stovetop until ready to serve.

To make the spaghetti, fill a large saucepan with water and bring to the boil. Add the parsnip strips and cook for 50 seconds until tender. Drain, toss with the olive oil and season with salt.

Divide the spaghetti between serving plates. Top with the meatballs, spoon on the tomato sauce and sprinkle with the parsley or basil leaves and grated macadamias.

Serves 4

One of the joys of my job is meeting the farmers and other people who produce the food we all enjoy. I was fortunate enough recently to spend a day in Tasmania at a wonderful cattle farm owned by John Bruce. While there I decided to cook heart, marrow and liver in three different recipes. Here is my liver recipe in all its glory. The key is to not overcook liver, but keep it lovely and pink inside.

PREP:
10 mins
COOK:
4 mins
(+ 2 mins to rest)

SPICED BEEF LIVER WITH AVOCADO SALAD

To make the Cajun spice mix, place all the ingredients in a bowl and mix until evenly blended.

Lightly coat the liver in 2 tablespoons of Cajun spice mix. (You can store the leftover Cajun spice mix in an airtight container in the pantry for a few months.)

Melt the oil or fat in a large frying pan over medium–high heat. Add the livers two at a time and cook, for 1½–2 minutes. Flip and cook for another 1½–2 minutes, until still slightly pink in the middle (or cook to your liking). Allow to rest, covered in foil, for a couple of minutes.

Meanwhile, to make the salad, place the avocado, coriander, chilli and walnuts in a bowl. In another bowl, mix the garlic, lemon juice and olive oil. Pour the dressing over the salad and gently toss. Season with salt and pepper.

Arrange the liver steaks on four plates, top with the avocado salad and garnish with the herbs and extra walnuts.

Serves 4

4 beef liver steaks (about 150 g each)
2 tablespoons coconut oil or other good-quality fat*
1 large handful of mixed flat-leaf parsley and coriander leaves, to serve

Cajun spice mix
2 teaspoons sea salt
2 teaspoons garlic powder
2 tablespoons paprika
1 teaspoon freshly ground black pepper
1 teaspoon onion powder
1 teaspoon cayenne pepper
1¼ teaspoons dried oregano
1¼ teaspoons dried thyme
½ teaspoon chilli flakes (optional)

Avocado salad
2 avocados, cut into 1 cm cubes
1 teaspoon finely chopped coriander leaves
1 long red chilli, deseeded and finely chopped
3½ tablespoons activated walnuts, toasted and crushed, plus extra to serve
1 garlic clove, finely chopped
3 tablespoons lemon juice
100 ml olive oil
sea salt and freshly ground black pepper

* See Glossary

Turn broccoli stems into stir-fry!

VEGGIE RICE ROCKS!

SIDES

Cauliflower
Bok choy
Chillies
Carrots
Asparagus

PREP:
10 mins
(+ 10 mins to stand)
COOK:
nil

Broccoli is a nutritional powerhouse that often features on our family table. I enjoy giving classic recipes a creative twist and wondered how I could jazz up broccoli, enhance its flavour and take it to another level. Then one day when I was looking at tabbouli I thought, why not mix finely chopped broccoli through this delicious salad? Success! I have used raw broccoli here but you could easily blanch or roast yours. This is a perfect accompaniment to grilled seafood or roast lamb or chicken.

BROCCOLI TABBOULI

500 g broccoli (about 1½ heads), cut into florets (reserve the stems for making stock)
4 tomatoes, deseeded and diced
2 large handfuls of flat-leaf parsley, chopped
½ red onion, diced
2 spring onions, finely sliced
2 tablespoons chia seeds*
freshly ground black pepper
sesame seeds, toasted, to serve

Dressing
2 garlic cloves, peeled
sea salt
4 tablespoons lemon juice
100 ml extra-virgin olive oil

* See Glossary

Place the broccoli in a food processor bowl and pulse until it resembles rice, then transfer to a large bowl. Stir through the tomato, parsley, red onion, spring onion and chia seeds and set aside.

To make the dressing, use a mortar and pestle to pound the garlic with a pinch of salt to form a thick paste. Add the lemon juice and olive oil and mix until well combined.

Add the dressing to the broccoli tabbouli and season with salt and pepper. Mix gently and allow to stand for 10 minutes so the flavours can develop.

Place the tabbouli in a large serving bowl and sprinkle with some sesame seeds.

Serves 4

Zucchini is one of those versatile vegetables that we always have in our fridge (well, actually it is a fruit but we commonly refer to it as a vegetable). Zucchini goes with just about anything and that is why I have created this very simple side dish. It works well alongside braises – think osso buco or lamb shank tagine – curries and even rich and delicious ragouts, such as bolognese sauce or the meat base in a shepherd's pie. You could serve this chilled in a salad with a mouth-watering dressing – vinaigrette or mayonnaise work well (or see the Basics chapter for more ideas).

ZUCCHINI RICE

2 large zucchini (about 500 g in total)
1 teaspoon coconut oil
sea salt (optional)

Slice the ends off the zucchini, then julienne with a mandoline or julienne peeler, or simply slice them into long, thin strips with a sharp knife.

Place the zucchini strips on a chopping board and dice into tiny pieces the size of rice grains.

Heat the oil in a wok or frying pan over medium heat. Add the zucchini rice and sauté for 5 minutes until softened. Season with salt, if desired.

Serves 4

CAULIFLOWER OR BROCCOLI RICE

You can make cauliflower or broccoli rice instead of zucchini rice if you'd prefer. Roughly chop 1 head of cauliflower or broccoli into florets, then place in a food processor and pulse into fine pieces that look like rice. Then proceed with the sautéing as above.

This simple broccoli dish, another of Michelle Tam from Nom Nom Paleo's creations, will, no doubt, become a staple in your home after you try it. It is the dish that got Michelle's kids eating broccoli – and all it took was to add some bacon. Genius! You can, of course, substitute cauliflower, mushrooms, pumpkin, asparagus or brussels sprouts – basically any vegetable – for the broccoli; that way you can have this whenever you like with whatever veggies are bountiful and in season. Team this with any piece of protein and you will have the easiest stress-free dinner ever.

PREP:
10 mins
COOK:
30 mins

ROASTED BROCCOLI AND BACON

Preheat the oven to 200°C.

Place the broccoli, garlic, bacon and oil or fat in a roasting tin and toss to combine. Season generously with salt and pepper and spread out in a single layer – do not overlap the broccoli or it may not brown properly. Roast in the oven for 30 minutes, rotating the tray and flipping the broccoli and bacon every 10 minutes.

Squeeze a little lemon juice or drizzle a splash of vinegar over the roasted broccoli for an extra boost of flavour just before serving, if you like.

Serves 4

2 heads of broccoli (about 600 g), cut into florets (reserve the stems for making soup or stock)
5 garlic cloves, roughly chopped
4 rashers of rindless bacon, cut into bite-sized pieces
2 tablespoons coconut oil or other good-quality fat*
sea salt and freshly ground black pepper
lemon juice or apple cider vinegar, to serve (optional)

* See Glossary

When cauliflowers are abundant and cheap I love to create new and exciting ways to prepare them. This fragrantly spiced cauliflower rice screams out to be served alongside an Indian curry, some Indian-style grilled fish or Indian roasted chicken (page 174). And if you want to complete your culinary adventure and take your meal to the next level, add some Indian-spiced fermented vegetables.

INDIAN CAULIFLOWER RICE

1 small cauliflower (about 600 g), florets and stalk roughly chopped
2 tablespoons coconut oil
2 teaspoons yellow or brown mustard seeds
12 fresh curry leaves (see note)
2 teaspoons cumin seeds
2 cinnamon sticks
2 small green chillies, deseeded and finely sliced
1 onion, finely chopped
2 garlic cloves, finely chopped
2 teaspoons curry powder
2 teaspoons ground turmeric
pinch of cayenne pepper (optional)
125 ml (½ cup) chicken, beef or vegetable stock or water
sea salt and freshly ground black pepper
activated cashew nuts or almonds, toasted, to serve (optional)

Place the cauliflower in a food processer bowl and pulse until it resembles rice. Do not over process as it will become mushy.

Melt the oil in a large frying pan or wok over medium–high heat. Add the mustard seeds, curry leaves, cumin seeds, cinnamon and half of the chilli and cook for 20 seconds until fragrant and lightly golden. Add the onion and garlic, then reduce the heat to medium and cook, stirring occasionally, for 5 minutes until the onion is translucent.

Add the curry power, turmeric and cayenne pepper (if using) and cook for a few seconds, then add the cauliflower rice and cook for 1 minute, tossing to coat. Pour in the stock or water and cook, tossing occasionally, for 3–4 minutes until the cauliflower is tender and the liquid has evaporated. Season with salt and pepper and serve with the extra chilli and some cashews or almonds if you like some crunch.

Serves 4

Note

Curry leaves come from the curry tree, which is native to India and Sri Lanka. They are available both fresh and dried from Asian grocers and some supermarkets. Fresh curry leaves freeze really well if sealed in a zip-lock bag.

PREP:
5 mins
COOK:
7 mins

Bok choy, a wonderfully nutrient-dense vegetable from the cabbage family, features in many Asian dishes. It is rich in antioxidants, phytonutrients, minerals and vitamins A, B-complex, C and K, making it a no-brainer for including it at your dinner table on a weekly basis. This simple side works well with grilled steak, steamed fish, five-spice roasted chicken, braised pork belly or beef short ribs. I encourage you to get bok choy on your plate, and when you are feeling adventurous, try fermenting it, too, by adding some to your kimchi.

BOK CHOY WITH GINGER

2 tablespoons coconut oil or other good-quality fat*

3 garlic cloves, finely chopped

4 cm piece of ginger, peeled and julienned

1 long red chilli, deseeded and sliced (optional)

3 heads of baby bok choy, trimmed

1½ tablespoons tamari or coconut aminos*

4 tablespoons chicken or vegetable stock, or water

1 teaspoon sesame oil

1 teaspoon sesame seeds, toasted

* See Glossary

Heat the oil or fat in a wok or large frying pan over medium–high heat. Add the garlic and ginger and sauté for 20 seconds, then add the remaining ingredients and stir-fry for 5–6 minutes, or until the bok choy is tender. Serve immediately.

Serves 4

I have travelled to Spain many times and love to order the classic tapas dish of fried padron peppers. The Spanish have a saying that one in ten will be extremely hot, so eating these bite-sized morsels is always a pleasurable adventure, especially if you like things spicy. In this recipe I wanted to show the respect I have for Spanish cuisine by teaming roasted chillies with a delicious romesco sauce – one of my favourites because it works with basically anything you can dream of. You can easily replace the chillies with roasted cauliflower, sweet potato, pumpkin, okra, asparagus or anything else that takes your fancy.

PREP:
15 mins
(+ 7 hrs to soak for
macadamia cheese)
COOK:
30 mins

ROASTED GREEN CHILLIES WITH ROMESCO SAUCE

Preheat the oven to 200°C.

To get started on the romesco sauce, place the capsicum, skin-side up, on a baking tray and roast for 30 minutes until the skin blisters and turns black. Transfer to a bowl, cover with plastic wrap and leave to cool for 5 minutes. Peel away and discard the skin and seeds, then chop the flesh.

Meanwhile, combine the tomato, chilli, paprika and coconut oil in a bowl and season with salt and pepper. Heat a frying pan over medium heat, add the tomato mixture and cook for 4 minutes until softened.

Place the chillies in a large roasting tin, drizzle over the oil and toss to evenly coat. Season with salt and pepper. Roast the chillies in the oven for 10–15 minutes until the skins are blackened and blistered. Flip the chillies over and roast for a further 5 minutes until softened.

Meanwhile, to finish the romesco sauce, place the hazelnuts and almonds in a food processor bowl and process until finely ground. Add the capsicum, tomato mixture, garlic and vinegar and process to a paste. With the motor running, slowly add the olive oil and process until well combined. Transfer to a bowl, cover with plastic wrap and refrigerate until needed.

Arrange the roasted chillies on a serving platter, scatter over the macadamia cheese and coriander leaves and finish with a squeeze of lime juice. Serve with the romesco sauce on the side.

Serves 4

12–14 long green chillies
1½–2 tablespoons coconut oil, melted

Romesco sauce
2 red capsicums, quartered
2 tomatoes, quartered
1 long red chilli, deseeded and chopped
1½ teaspoons smoked paprika
1 tablespoon coconut oil, melted
sea salt and freshly ground black pepper
12 activated hazelnuts, lightly toasted
12 activated almonds, lightly toasted
3 garlic cloves, chopped
2 tablespoons apple cider vinegar
4 tablespoons extra-virgin olive oil

To serve
120 g Macadamia Cheese (page 256) (optional)
1 handful of coriander leaves
1 lime, halved

TIP

This recipe is a spicy dish and is recommended for chilli lovers. It is a perfect side for beef, lamb, pork and fish dishes.

So much precious food is wasted **each year, we really need to be** far more mindful about how to **best use it. And with food prices** escalating it makes perfect sense that we utilise as much as we can of the ingredients we choose. That is where this clever little recipe comes into play, as we are actually turning the broccoli stem, which usually goes into the compost bin or feeds the chickens, into the hero of this wonderful side dish. If you wanted to turn it into a main course for the **whole family, add some prawns,** chicken, beef or lamb. I can't **wait to hear what you think of it.**

BROCCOLI STEM STIR-FRY

4 thick broccoli stems
1 large carrot
2 large zucchini
2 tablespoons coconut oil
2 garlic cloves, finely chopped
½ teaspoon finely grated ginger
120 g snow peas, tailed and
    julienned
2 long red chillies, deseeded and
    julienned
2 spring onions, finely sliced
2 tablespoons tamari or coconut
    aminos*
3 tablespoons chicken stock or
    water
1 tablespoon sugar-free chilli
    sauce (optional)
2 teaspoons sesame oil
sea salt and freshly ground black
    pepper
1 tablespoon lime juice
sesame seeds, toasted, to serve
lime wedges, to serve

See Glossary

Trim and discard any leaves or woody parts on the broccoli stems.

Use a veggie spiraliser to make noodles from the broccoli stems, carrot and zucchini.

Heat a wok or large saucepan over high heat. Add the coconut oil, garlic and ginger and fry for 20 seconds until just starting to brown. Add the broccoli, carrot, zucchini, snow peas, chilli and spring onion. Toss well and cook for 2 minutes. Add the tamari or coconut aminos, stock or water, chilli sauce (if using) and sesame oil, then toss well and continue to cook for a further 2 minutes.

Season the broccoli mixture with a little salt and pepper. Add the lime juice, then toss again and sprinkle with the sesame seeds. Serve with the lime wedges on the side.

Serves 4

TIP

If you don't have a veggie spiraliser, use a vegetable peeler to shave the broccoli stems, carrot and zucchini lengthways, or finely slice them with a sharp knife. Cut each slice again lengthways into thin, noodle-like strips.

When the warmer weather starts, you will find our family eating outdoors with me at my favourite place, manning the barbecue. We all have that picture of steaks and snags filling up the barbecue; you never see a barbie full of veggies. And that is just what I want to promote, as the flavour from barbecuing your veggies is second to none. To turn this side dish into a wonderful and nutritious meal, add some fermented veggies on the side and throw in a couple of good-quality snags, a beautiful piece of seafood or some lamb chops.

BARBECUED BALSAMIC VEGGIES

1 red capsicum, cut into 1 cm strips
2 zucchini, cut into 1 cm strips lengthways
6 Dutch carrots, halved lengthways
6 asparagus spears, woody ends trimmed, halved lengthways
1 sweet potato, sliced into 5 mm rounds
1 red onion, cut into wedges
2 portobello mushrooms, sliced
4 baby beetroot, roasted and halved (optional)
1 garlic bulb, halved crossways
6 spring onions, trimmed
3 tablespoons coconut oil or other good-quality fat*, melted
sea salt and freshly ground black pepper
Aioli (page 242), to serve

Dressing
3 tablespoons balsamic vinegar
4 tablespoons extra-virgin olive oil

* See Glossary

To make the dressing, whisk the balsamic vinegar and olive oil together in a small bowl.

Heat a barbecue plate or chargrill pan to medium–high.

Brush the vegetables with the oil or fat and season with salt and pepper. Working in batches, cook the vegetables until tender and charred all over, turning occasionally.

Arrange the grilled vegetables on a serving platter. Drizzle the dressing over the vegetables and serve with some aioli on the side.

Serves 4–6

Bananas
Coconuts
Chocolate
Apples
Cherries

HEALTHY
TREATS
ARE EASY
TO MAKE!

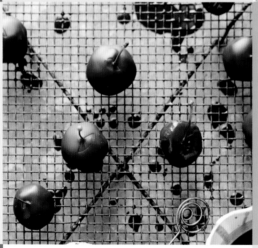

MIX, BEAT, BAKE, SAVOUR!

TREATS

Enjoy a herbal tea after dinner

My goal as a paleo chef is to reinterpret family favourites and remove ingredients that have a negative impact on our health. By simply replacing white flour with coconut or nut flour, butter with coconut oil and refined sugar with stevia, honey, yacon or maple syrup, we can still bake cookies or a cake for a birthday celebration and know that what is on offer is delicious but, more importantly, so much easier on our systems. These little rippers will fly out the door at your next party, school fete or work fundraiser.

COCONUT MACAROONS

2 eggwhites
pinch of sea salt
pinch of cream of tartar
¼ teaspoon apple cider vinegar
2 tablespoons honey
50 g (scant ½ cup) almond meal
1 tablespoon melted coconut oil
100 g (1⅔ cups) shredded coconut
200 g cherries, pitted and chopped

Preheat the oven to 160°C and line a large tray with baking paper.

Beat the eggwhites and salt in a bowl until soft peaks form. Add the cream of tartar, vinegar and honey and continue to beat until thick and glossy. Fold in the almond meal, coconut oil, shredded coconut and cherries.

Using a tablespoon, drop walnut-sized portions of the macaroon mixture onto the prepared tray, allowing a little room for spreading. Bake for 12–15 minutes until the macaroons are golden brown. Allow the macaroons to cool a little before transferring to a wire rack to cool completely. Store in an airtight container in the cupboard for up to a week.

Makes 16

In my teenage years, one of my first jobs as an apprentice was working in a fancy cafe and every day I made muffins for customers to have with their coffee. Banana muffins were one of my favourites, as they not only had the most amazing flavour but were always moist and well loved by the guests. This version, my paleo take on the classic banana muffin, will be equally as loved as the ones I used to make 25 years ago.

BANANA MUFFINS

200 g (2 cups) almond meal
60 g tapioca flour*
1½ teaspoons bicarbonate
   of soda
¼ teaspoon sea salt
115 g (⅓ cup) honey
3 tablespoons coconut oil,
   at room temperature
1½ teaspoons vanilla powder
3 large eggs, at room temperature
125 ml (½ cup) almond milk
4 ripe bananas

See Glossary

Preheat the oven to 180°C. Line a 12-cup muffin tin with paper cases.

Combine the almond meal, tapioca flour, bicarbonate of soda and salt in a bowl. Use a fork to crush any almond meal clumps, then mix to a fine crumb.

Using an electric mixer on medium speed, beat the honey and oil for 2–4 minutes, or until creamy. Add the vanilla and eggs and continue beating for a further 1–2 minutes until well combined. Add the almond meal mixture and beat to combine. Slowly mix in the almond milk with a wooden spoon until just combined.

Mash three of the bananas with a fork and gently fold into the batter. Divide the batter between the paper cases. Cut the remaining banana into 12 slices and place one on top of each muffin. Bake for 25 minutes, until the tops are golden brown and a toothpick inserted in the centre of a muffin comes out clean.

Transfer the muffins to a wire rack and allow to cool before serving. Store in an airtight container in the fridge for up to 5 days, or in the freezer for up to 3 months.

Makes 12

Ice blocks were my favourite childhood treat on a hot summer's day. The moment I popped one in my mouth, the refreshing feeling made me smile from ear to ear. I wanted to create a frozen treat that my kids and others would love. Young coconut makes the perfect base ingredient, as it is sweet, without being overly sweet, has a good nutritional profile and is great for rehydration. I've also added tart pomegranate juice, which is full of health benefits – it aids digestion, is anti-ageing and boosts immunity. A single glass of freshly made pomegranate juice can provide 40 per cent of your daily requirements of folic acid and vitamins A, C and E.

PREP:
10 mins
(+ 5 hrs to freeze)
COOK:
nil

POMEGRANATE AND COCONUT POPSICLES

Remove about 3 tablespoons of seeds from one of the pomegranate halves and set aside.

Open the coconut by cutting a hole in the top. Pour the coconut water into a measuring cup; you should get about 250 ml. Divide the coconut water between eight popsicle moulds so that each is half full. (Reserve the coconut flesh for another use, such as adding to smoothies.)

Add a few pomegranate seeds to each mould and freeze for 1 hour. Insert a popsicle stick in each mould and return to the freezer for another hour.

Using a manual citrus juicer, squeeze and press each of the pomegranate halves in a circular motion until all the juice is released.

Line a colander with muslin and strain the pomegranate juice; you should get about 125 ml of juice from each pomegranate. Stir in the honey, adding more, if desired.

Pour the pomegranate juice into the popsicle moulds and return to the freezer for 4 hours, or until frozen.

Makes 8

3 pomegranates, halved
1 young green coconut*
1 tablespoon honey, or to taste

* See Glossary

TIP

When buying pomegranates, choose ones that are heavy as they contain the most juice.

Warming drinks in a flash

Need to focus and concentrate?
Rosemary, ginkgo, gotu kola and peppermint have all been shown to improve cognitive function, lift mood and increase blood flow to the brain. These herbs can all be purchased in dried form from health food stores – Southern Light Herbs is a great organic brand. Simply infuse any combination of these in hot water for 5 minutes, then strain and serve.

I often make up a simple digestif that I drink 20 minutes or so after a meal. Simply mix dried fennel leaves, chamomile flowers, spearmint leaves and crushed cardamom pods, then infuse in hot water for 5 minutes. Strain and enjoy.

To make a healthy paleo hot chocolate, place some coconut milk in a saucepan with a pinch each of ground cinnamon and vanilla powder and heat gently. Once the milk is hot, remove from the heat and add a couple of squares of raw dark chocolate (80% cacao and no refined sugar). Whisk until completely melted then enjoy.

Warm nut milk is such a treat on a winter's night (see page 16 for instructions on making your own nut milk). One of my favourite combinations is hazelnut milk warmed with some grated nutmeg, ground cinnamon and a touch of stevia. I also love macadamia milk heated with a sprinkling of vanilla powder, cardamom pods, cloves, star anise and a cinnamon stick. Once warm, strain the whole spices out and enjoy.

To make a delicious ginseng tea, place some dried ginseng, chopped fresh lemongrass, a cinnamon stick and a few crushed cardamom pods in a saucepan. Add 750 ml of filtered water and bring to the boil over medium–high heat. Reduce the heat to medium–low and simmer for 10–15 minutes. Strain and serve with a little manuka honey, if desired. This tea is also delicious served chilled over ice.

Brownies are one of those treats that disappear very, very quickly, especially if they are teamed with a lovely hot chocolate on the side (made with coconut or hazelnut milk, of course). As I have said many times throughout this book, paleo is not about going without; rather it is about making wise choices with the foods we consume to help us live happier and healthier lives. By replacing refined white flour, dairy and sugar with paleo alternatives, we can lessen the impact treats have on our systems while still enjoying the good things in life. I guarantee that when you try these you will see that you are in no way missing out on anything.

CHOCOLATE BROWNIES

200 g raw dark chocolate
(at least 80% cacao, with no
refined sugar), chopped
185 ml (¾ cup) coconut oil
3 tablespoons cacao powder,
plus 2 tablespoons extra
to dust
6 eggs, separated
300 g honey
200 g (2 cups) activated walnuts,
toasted and roughly chopped

Preheat the oven to 160°C. Grease an 18 cm × 28 cm baking tin and line the base and sides with baking paper.

Combine the chocolate, coconut oil and cacao powder in a heatproof bowl set over (but not touching) a saucepan of just-simmering water. Stir the chocolate mixture occasionally with a spatula until melted and smooth. Remove from the heat and set aside to cool slightly.

Meanwhile, combine the egg yolks and 175 g of the honey in a bowl and beat on high speed with an electric mixer until doubled in size and fluffy. Fold the egg yolk mixture into the chocolate mixture with a metal spoon.

Whisk the eggwhites and the remaining honey in a large bowl until soft peaks form. Fold the eggwhite mixture into the chocolate mixture until well incorporated, then gently fold in the walnuts.

Pour the brownie mixture into the prepared tin and level the top with a palette knife. Bake for 30 minutes, or until a skewer inserted in the centre of the brownie comes out clean. The brownie will puff up a little during cooking. Allow to cool completely in the tin, then refrigerate for 2 hours before cutting.

Turn the brownie out onto a chopping board and cut into portions. Dust with the extra cacao powder and serve. The brownies will keep in an airtight container in the fridge for up to 5 days.

Makes 16–20 pieces

To me, there's nothing better on a cold winter's night than apple crumble. And if you are going to indulge in a dessert, then a paleo version is always a better choice. What is so brilliant about this dish is how my paleo makeover has made the traditional crumble tastier and more enjoyable. Use whatever organic or chemical-free fruit you can get your hands on and go for gold. Remember to exercise restraint with dishes like this and only have them every once in a while.

APPLE AND BERRY CRUMBLE

4 apples (about 750 g in total), peeled, cored and chopped into 2 cm pieces
85 g (scant ¼ cup) honey
1 tablespoon coconut oil
finely grated zest of 1 orange
1 teaspoon ground cinnamon
½ teaspoon vanilla powder or 1 vanilla pod, split and seeds scraped
320 g fresh or frozen mixed berries (such as blueberries, raspberries, strawberries, blackberries)
coconut yoghurt, to serve

Crumble topping
100 g (1 cup) almond or hazelnut meal
65 g (½ cup) activated macadamia nuts, finely chopped
60 g (½ cup) activated pistachio nuts, finely chopped
40 g (⅔ cup) shredded coconut
4 tablespoons coconut oil, melted
85 g (scant ¼ cup) honey
½ teaspoon ground cinnamon
pinch of sea salt

Preheat the oven to 160°C.

To make the filling, combine the apple, honey, coconut oil, orange zest, cinnamon, vanilla pod and seeds or powder and 3 tablespoons of water in a saucepan. Cover and cook over medium–low heat, stirring occasionally, until the apple softens, about 5 minutes. Add the berries, cover and cook for 3–4 minutes until the berries start to burst. Remove the vanilla pod (if using).

Meanwhile, to make the crumble topping, place all the ingredients in a bowl and mix well.

Spoon the filling evenly into a 1.5 litre baking dish. Sprinkle on the crumble topping to cover. Bake for 15–18 minutes until the crumble is golden brown, checking from 10 minutes onwards to make sure it doesn't burn. Remove from the oven and allow to stand for 2–3 minutes before serving. Serve with coconut yoghurt.

Serves 6

The Cherry Ripe would have to be one of our most famous chocolate bars. This delicious chocolate-coated cherry and coconut mixture can, in all honesty, be made quite healthy – and I am going to show you how. This version is free of artificial colourings and flavourings, soy, dairy, vegetable oils, emulsifiers, refined sugars (and who knows what else) and contains only real ingredients that you can feel safe serving to your family.

PREP:
15 mins
(+ 35 mins to chill)
COOK:
20 mins

'CHERRY RIPE' BITES

Preheat the oven to 160°C. Line two baking trays with baking paper.

Place the cherries on one of the trays and bake for 15 minutes. (Keep the cherry stems aside in a separate bowl.) Allow the cherries to cool for about 5 minutes.

Place the baked cherries, honey, dates, coconut and oil in a food processor bowl and pulse briefly until the mixture comes together.

Roll the mixture into cherry-sized balls and insert a cherry stem in the centre of each ball. Place on the other lined tray, transfer to the freezer and chill for 30 minutes, or until firm.

Meanwhile, place the chocolate in a heatproof bowl over a saucepan of just-simmering water and stir until the chocolate is melted. Remove from the heat and dip the chilled cherry balls into the chocolate until they are completely coated, then return them to the paper-lined tray. Transfer the tray to the fridge and chill for 5 minutes to set the chocolate. Store in an airtight container in the fridge for up to 1 week.

Makes 22–24

200 g cherries, pitted and halved, stems reserved (80 g when pitted)
1 tablespoon honey
2 fresh dates, pitted
90 g (1 cup) desiccated coconut
3 tablespoons coconut oil, melted
250 g raw dark chocolate (at least 80% cacao, with no refined sugar), chopped

What a novel way to get raw beetroot into your diet! These delectable mud cakes were created because of my dear friend, nutritional biochemist Dr Libby Weaver, one of the most inspiring women on the planet. Dr Libby speaks the same language I do: that food can be medicine or it can be a form of poison for our bodies and minds. Dr Libby would agree that treats like this should be enjoyed from time to time and in moderation, so save these for a very special occasion.

CHOCOLATE AND BEETROOT MUD CAKES

300 g (2 cups) mixed activated macadamia nuts and Brazil nuts
6 medjool dates, pitted
55 g (¼ cup) currants, dried blueberries or dried cranberries
4 tablespoons maple syrup
3 beetroot, grated, plus extra to decorate
200 g (2¼ cups) desiccated coconut, plus extra to decorate
4 tablespoons cacao powder
4 tablespoons carob powder
½ teaspoon vanilla powder or 1 vanilla pod, split and seeds scraped
2 tablespoons golden flaxseed meal*

Icing
2 avocados, halved, stoned and peeled
60 g (½ cup) cacao powder
175 g (½ cup) honey
2 tablespoons coconut oil
½ teaspoon vanilla powder
½ teaspoon sea salt

Chocolate shavings
125 ml (½ cup) melted coconut oil
1½ tablespoons cacao powder, sifted
1½ tablespoons carob powder, sifted
1 tablespoon honey

See Glossary

Place the nuts in a food processor bowl and process to the consistency of breadcrumbs. Add the dates, dried fruit and maple syrup and process until smooth. Add the beetroot, coconut, cacao, carob, vanilla powder or seeds and flaxseed meal and blend until well combined and even in texture.

Line a tray with baking paper. Place eight 5 cm cake ring moulds on the tray. Divide the nut mixture between the moulds and transfer to the freezer for 40 minutes to set.

To make the icing, combine the avocado, cacao, honey, coconut oil, vanilla and salt in the clean food processor bowl and pulse until smooth.

Using a palette knife, cover the cakes with the icing, then refrigerate for 30 minutes.

Meanwhile, to make the chocolate shavings, mix the coconut oil, cacao, carob and honey in a bowl. Line a tray with baking paper and spread the mixture onto the paper as thinly as possible. Leave at room temperature for 5 minutes, then carefully roll up the paper to form a cylinder. Place in the fridge for 10–20 minutes to harden. Peel the paper away; you will be left with chocolate shavings. Place these on the baking sheet and return to the fridge for 2–5 minutes to firm up again.

Decorate the mud cakes with the extra coconut and beetroot and the chocolate shavings. Store in an airtight container in the fridge for up to 5 days.

Makes 8

HOMEMADE SAUCES TASTE BETTER!

Cook up a storm on the weekend

BASICS

Mayo
Dressings
Relishes
Sauces
Paleo bread

BASICS ARE THE KEY TO GOOD COOKING!

MAYONNAISE

4 egg yolks
2 teaspoons Dijon mustard
1 tablespoon apple cider vinegar
1 tablespoon lemon juice
sea salt
400 ml olive oil or macadamia oil
freshly ground black pepper

Place the egg yolks, mustard, vinegar, lemon juice and a pinch of salt in a food processor bowl or blender jug and process until combined. With the motor running, slowly pour in the oil in a thin stream and process until the mayonnaise is thick and creamy. Season with salt and pepper. Store in a glass jar in the fridge for 4–5 days.

Makes about 500 g

AIOLI

To make aioli, simply add 1 crushed garlic clove to the ingredients and proceed with the recipe as above.

You can play around by adding different fresh herbs to your aioli – try basil, coriander, dill or whatever herb you love. Roughly chop the leaves and add to the food processor along with the rest of the ingredients.

PREP:
10 mins
(+ 30 mins to soak
& 5 mins to cool)
cook:
23 mins

BEETROOT HARISSA

40 g dried chillies
2 long red chillies
½ teaspoon caraway seeds
½ teaspoon coriander seeds
½ teaspoon cumin seeds
4 garlic cloves, peeled
4 tablespoons olive oil
1 large beetroot (about 150 g),
   grated
2 tablespoons lemon juice
½ teaspoon sea salt

Preheat the oven to 200°C.

Place the dried chillies in a bowl and cover with hot water. Soak for 30 minutes. Drain.

Meanwhile, put the fresh chillies on a baking tray and roast for 20 minutes, or until blackened and blistered. Remove from the oven and put in a brown paper bag or wrap in paper towel to cool for 5 minutes. Scrape away the charred skin, remove the seeds, roughly chop and place in a food processor bowl.

Lightly toast the caraway, coriander and cumin seeds in a dry frying pan over medium heat until aromatic, about 3 minutes. Grind in a spice grinder or mortar and pestle, then add to the food processor.

Remove the seeds from the soaked chillies (make sure you wear gloves!) and add to the food processor.

Place all the remaining ingredients in the food processor bowl and pulse until well combined and smooth. Store in a glass jar in the fridge for up to 2 weeks.

Makes about 300 g

PREP:
5 mins
COOK:
nil

OLIVE TAPENADE

Put everything except the oil into a food processor bowl and process until well combined. With the motor running, drizzle in the oil until you get a nice thick paste consistency. Store in a glass jar in the fridge for up to 2 weeks.

Makes about 185 g

125 g pitted black or green olives
juice and zest of ½ lemon
8 basil leaves
2 garlic cloves, peeled
½ small red chilli, deseeded and
   chopped
2 salted anchovy fillets, rinsed
   and patted dry
10 salted baby capers, rinsed
   well and patted dry
3 tablespoons olive oil

PALEO BUNS

300 g (3 cups) almond meal
55 g (heaped ½ cup) psyllium husks*
1 tablespoon coconut flour
1 tablespoon bicarbonate of soda
½ teaspoon sea salt
4 tablespoons apple cider vinegar
2 teaspoons honey
375 ml (1½ cups) boiling water
6 eggwhites, whisked

* See Glossary

Preheat the oven to 180°C and line a baking tray with baking paper.

Place the dry ingredients in a large bowl and mix well.

Combine the vinegar, honey and boiling water in a glass jug.

Fold the eggwhites into the dry ingredients. Pour in the vinegar mixture and stir vigorously. The mixture will froth up. Keep mixing for 30 seconds until it forms a very thick batter. Knead with your hands until the batter becomes a sticky dough.

Working quickly so the dough doesn't dry out, divide into eight portions and shape into balls, then place on the prepared tray, a few centimetres apart. Bake in the oven for 50 minutes until golden brown and a roll sounds hollow when the base is tapped. Allow to cool on a wire rack before serving. Store in an airtight container in the fridge for up to 5 days, or in the freezer for up to 3 months.

Makes 8

BACON AND SHERRY VINAIGRETTE

1 tablespoon coconut oil
½ French shallot, finely chopped
120 g rindless bacon, finely diced
4 tablespoons sherry vinegar or
    apple cider vinegar
1 teaspoon Dijon mustard
1 teaspoon finely snipped chives
100 ml extra-virgin olive oil
sea salt and freshly ground
    black pepper

Heat half of the coconut oil in a small saucepan over low heat. Add the shallot and cook for 5 minutes until soft. Remove from the pan.

Add the remaining coconut oil and the bacon to the pan and fry over medium heat, stirring occasionally, for 6–8 minutes, or until the bacon is golden. Stir in the vinegar and shallot and set aside for about 5 minutes to cool.

Transfer the bacon and shallot mixture to a bowl and whisk in the mustard, chives and olive oil and season with salt and pepper. Store in a glass jar in the fridge for up to 1 week. Shake well before using.

Makes about 250 ml

GREEN GODDESS DRESSING

½ avocado
3 tablespoons coconut milk
3 tablespoons lemon juice
1 garlic clove, finely chopped
2 anchovy fillets, finely chopped
½ cup chopped flat-leaf
    parsley leaves
3 tablespoons chopped basil
    leaves
1 tablespoon chopped tarragon
    leaves
¼ teaspoon salt
125 ml (½ cup) extra-virgin
    olive oil

Place all of the ingredients except the oil in a food processor bowl and process until well combined. With the motor running, slowly pour in the oil and process until the dressing thickens and the herbs are finely chopped. Store in a glass jar in the fridge for up to 5 days.

Makes about 250 ml

BEETROOT CHIMICHURRI

PREP:
10 mins

Combine the beetroot, oil, parsley, basil, tarragon, onion, garlic, cumin, paprika, vinegar and chilli in a food processer bowl and pulse until finely chopped. Add a little more oil if the sauce is too thick. Season with salt and pepper. Store in a glass jar in the fridge for up to 1 week.

Makes 600 g

1 large beetroot, peeled and grated
250 ml (1 cup) extra-virgin olive oil, plus extra if needed
2 very large handfuls of flat-leaf parsley leaves
2 handfuls of basil leaves
2 tablespoons chopped tarragon leaves
½ red onion, chopped
2 garlic cloves, finely chopped
½ teaspoon ground cumin
¼ teaspoon smoked paprika
4 tablespoons apple cider vinegar or red wine vinegar
¼ long red chilli, deseeded and finely chopped
sea salt and freshly ground black pepper

CHIMICHURRI

PREP:
5 mins

Place the garlic, chilli and herbs in a food processor bowl and pulse to a fine paste. Add the vinegar, smoked paprika, cumin and oil and pulse to combine. Taste and season with salt and pepper. Set aside until needed. Store in a glass jar in the fridge for up to 5 days.

Makes about 250 ml

3 garlic cloves, peeled and roughly chopped
1 jalapeno chilli, deseeded and chopped
1 very large handful each of flat-leaf parsley and coriander leaves (about 15 g each), roughly chopped
1 small handful of oregano leaves (about 5 g), roughly chopped
1 tablespoon thyme leaves
100 ml apple cider vinegar
½ tablespoon smoked paprika
½ teaspoon ground cumin
150 ml olive oil or macadamia oil
sea salt and freshly ground black pepper

HERB AND GARLIC VINAIGRETTE

125 ml (½ cup) extra-virgin olive oil
3 tablespoons apple cider vinegar
2 tablespoons finely chopped mixed herbs (such as chervil, flat-leaf parsley, dill, tarragon)
1 garlic clove, finely chopped
pinch of sea salt

Combine all the ingredients in a screw-top glass jar. Screw the lid on firmly and shake well. Use immediately or store in the fridge for up to 3 days. Shake well before using.

Makes 185 ml

MUSTARD VINAIGRETTE

4 tablespoons apple cider vinegar or lemon juice
2 tablespoons wholegrain mustard
1 teaspoon sea salt
¼ teaspoon freshly ground black pepper
1 garlic clove, finely chopped
250 ml (1 cup) extra-virgin olive oil or macadamia oil

Combine all the ingredients in a screw-top jar. Screw the lid on firmly and shake well. Store in the fridge for up to 5 days. Shake well before using.

Makes 400 ml

HERB AND ANCHOVY DRESSING

PREP:
5 mins

Put the parsley, dill, chives, anchovies and vinegar in a food processor bowl or high-speed blender jug and process until combined. With the motor running, slowly pour in the oil and process until smooth. Pour the dressing into a bowl and season with salt and pepper. Store in the fridge for up to 3 days.

Makes 435 ml

- 2 large handfuls of flat-leaf parsley leaves, roughly chopped
- 1 handful of dill fronds, roughly chopped
- 3 tablespoons snipped chives
- 2 salted anchovy fillets, rinsed and patted dry
- 2 tablespoons apple cider vinegar
- 375 ml (1½ cups) extra-virgin olive oil
- sea salt and freshly ground black pepper

NAM JIM DRESSING

PREP:
7 mins

Place the shallot, chilli, garlic, ginger and coriander root in a food processor bowl and process to form a paste. Add the lime juice and fish sauce and pulse to combine. Taste and adjust the seasoning if necessary so that the dressing is a balance of hot, sour, salty and sweet.

Strain the dressing through a sieve and discard the pulp. Store in a glass jar in the fridge for up to a week. Shake well before using.

Makes about 200 ml

- 4 red Asian shallots, chopped
- 2 long red chillies, seeded and chopped
- 2 garlic cloves, chopped
- 2.5 cm piece of ginger, peeled and chopped
- 1 teaspoon chopped coriander roots
- 150 ml lime juice
- 2½ tablespoons fish sauce

BEEF BONE BROTH

2 kg beef knuckle and marrow
bones
1 cow's foot, cut into pieces
(optional)
3 tablespoons apple cider
vinegar
1.5 kg meaty beef rib or
neck bones
3 onions, roughly chopped
3 carrots, roughly chopped
3 celery stalks, roughly chopped
2 leeks, white part only, rinsed
well and roughly chopped
3 thyme sprigs
2 bay leaves
1 teaspoon black peppercorns,
crushed
1 garlic bulb, cut in half
horizontally
2 large handfuls of flat-leaf
parsley (stalks and leaves)

Place the knuckle and marrow bones and cow's foot (if using) in
a stockpot or very large saucepan. Add the vinegar and pour in
5 litres of cold water, or enough to cover. Let stand for 1 hour to
help draw out the nutrients from the bones. Remove the bones,
reserving the water.

Preheat the oven to 180°C.

Place the knuckle and marrow bones, cow's foot (if using) and
meaty bones in a few large roasting tins and roast in the oven for
30 minutes, or until well browned. Add all the bones to the stockpot
or pan along with the vegetables.

Pour the fat out of the roasting tins into a saucepan. Add 1 litre of
the reserved water, place over high heat and bring to a simmer,
stirring with a wooden spoon to loosen any coagulated juices. Add
this liquid to the bones and vegetables. Add the additional reserved
water to just cover the bones; the liquid should come no higher than
2 cm below the rim of the pan, as the volume will expand slightly
during cooking.

Bring the broth to the boil, skimming off the scum that rises to
the top. Reduce the heat to low and add the thyme, bay leaves,
peppercorns and garlic. Simmer for 12–24 hours (the longer you
leave the broth to simmer, the darker and richer it will become). Just
before finishing, add the parsley and simmer for another 10 minutes.
Strain the broth into a large container. Cover and cool in the fridge.
Remove the congealed fat that rises to the top. Transfer the bone
broth to smaller airtight containers and place in the fridge or, for
long-term storage, the freezer. The broth can be stored in the fridge
for 3–4 days or frozen for up to 3 months.

Makes 3½–4 litres

SALSA VERDE

Combine all the ingredients in a food processor bowl and blitz to form a thick paste. Keep the salsa verde in a glass jar in the fridge for up to 1 week.

Makes about 500 g

PREP:
5 mins

250 ml (1 cup) extra-virgin
   olive oil
2 handfuls each of basil, mint and
   flat-leaf parsley leaves
2 garlic cloves, chopped
4 salted anchovy fillets, rinsed
   and patted dry
50 g salted baby capers, rinsed
   and patted dry
1 tablespoon finely chopped
   cornichons (optional)
1 tablespoon lemon juice
50 g (⅓ cup) pine nuts, toasted
sea salt and freshly ground
   black pepper

TOMATO RELISH

PREP:
10 mins
COOK:
26 mins

Heat the coconut oil in a saucepan over medium heat. Add the onion and cook for a few minutes until lightly browned. Add the mustard seeds, garlic, chilli, ginger and turmeric and cook for 1 minute, or until fragrant and the mustard seeds start to pop.

Add the tomato to the pan and cook for 5 minutes, or until softened. Stir in the vinegar and honey (if using) and simmer, stirring regularly, for 20 minutes, or until the liquid is reduced by half. Season with salt and pepper, then transfer to a sterilised jar and store in the fridge for up to 2 months.

Makes 500 g

1 tablespoon coconut oil
1 onion, finely chopped
1 tablespoon yellow mustard
   seeds
3 garlic cloves, chopped
1 long red chilli, chopped
1 tablespoon grated ginger
1 tablespoon ground turmeric
6 tomatoes, diced
3 tablespoons red wine vinegar
   or apple cider vinegar
3 tablespoons honey (optional)
sea salt and freshly ground black
   pepper

3 tablespoons sunflower seeds, chopped, plus extra for sprinkling
3 tablespoons pumpkin seeds, chopped, plus extra for sprinkling
1 tablespoon chia seeds*, plus extra for sprinkling
50 g (⅓ cup) activated almonds, chopped
150 g (1½ cups) almond meal
3 tablespoons LSA
1 teaspoon bicarbonate of soda
2 tablespoons coconut flour
6 eggs, whisked
1 tablespoon honey (optional)
1 tablespoon apple cider vinegar
4 tablespoons coconut oil
1 teaspoon sea salt

*See Glossary

320 g macadamia nuts
1–1½ tablespoons lemon juice
1 teaspoon sea salt
pinch of freshly ground black pepper

SEED AND NUT BREAD

Preheat the oven to 160°C. Grease a 20 cm × 10 cm loaf tin and line the base and sides with baking paper.

Combine the sunflower, pumpkin and chia seeds in a large bowl. Stir through the almonds, almond meal, LSA, bicarbonate of soda and coconut flour. Add the eggs, honey (if using), vinegar, coconut oil and salt and mix well to combine. The mixture will resemble a batter rather than a dough.

Pour the dough into the prepared loaf tin and smooth out evenly with a spatula. Sprinkle the extra seeds on top (about 1 tablespoon of each is great). Bake for 45–50 minutes, or until golden and a skewer inserted in the centre comes out clean. (You will need to do the skewer test because this bread is much more dense than regular bread and won't sound hollow when you tap it.) Remove from the oven and allow to cool in the tin before turning out. Store in an airtight container in the fridge for up to 5 days, or in the freezer for up to 3 months.

Makes 1 loaf

MACADAMIA CHEESE

Soak the macadamia nuts in 750 ml of water for 6 hours. Drain and rinse well.

Place the nuts in a food processor with the lemon juice, salt and pepper and pulse for 1 minute to combine. Add 120 ml of water and process until smooth. If it seems a little dry, add more water and lemon juice to adjust the consistency. The macadamia cheese can be stored in an airtight container in the fridge for up to 1 week.

Makes about 600 g

CASHEW CHEESE

You can use cashews instead of macadamias if you prefer. Follow the recipe as above – the only difference is that they may require less water than the macadamias to reach the right consistency.

NIC'S PALEO BREAD

PREP:
10 mins
COOK:
1 hr 20 mins

Preheat the oven to 140°C. Grease a 20 cm × 10 cm loaf tin and line the base and sides with baking paper.

Combine all the dry ingredients in a large bowl. Add the eggs, vinegar and olive oil and stir well.

Spoon the mixture into the prepared tin and spread out evenly. Bake for 1 hour and 20 minutes, or until a skewer inserted in the centre comes out clean. Remove from the oven and allow to cool a little in the tin before turning out onto a wire rack. Store in an airtight container in the fridge for up to 5 days, or in the freezer for up to 3 months.

Serves 6

150 g (1½ cups) almond meal, sifted
50 g (½ cup) coconut flour, sifted
6 tablespoons psyllium seed powder*
1 tablespoon baking powder
a few good pinches of sea salt
12 eggs, lightly beaten
1½ tablespoons apple cider vinegar
120 ml extra-virgin olive oil

* See Glossary

COCONUT PITA BREADS

PREP:
5 mins
COOK:
15 mins

Whisk the coconut flour, tapioca flour, almond meal, salt, eggwhites and 125 ml of water in a large bowl to make a smooth batter.

Melt 1 teaspoon of the coconut oil in a small frying pan over medium–high heat. Pour about 3 tablespoons of batter into the pan. Slightly tilt and swirl the pan to spread the batter into a thin circle, about 13 cm in diameter. Cook for a few minutes, or until golden brown, then flip and cook on the other side until lightly golden. Transfer to a plate and keep warm. Repeat this process until you have used up all the batter. Store in an airtight container in the fridge for up to 5 days.

Makes 8

3 tablespoons coconut flour
3 tablespoons tapioca flour*
2 tablespoons almond meal
½ teaspoon fine sea salt
8 large eggwhites
2 tablespoons coconut oil

* See Glossary

SAUERKRAUT WITH DILL AND JUNIPER BERRIES

1 star anise
1 teaspoon whole cloves
600 g cabbage (you can use savoy or red, or a mixture of the two)
1½ teaspoons sea salt
3 tablespoons chopped dill
2 tablespoons juniper berries (see note)
1 sachet vegetable starter culture (this will weigh 2–5 g, depending on the brand) (see note)
1 handful of dill tips, to serve

Note

Juniper berries are purple in colour and are most famous for lending their flavour to gin. They can be found at some health food stores, specialty food stores or online. Vegetable starter culture can be used to kick-start the fermentation process when culturing veggies and is available from health food stores or online.

You will need a 1.5-litre preserving jar with an airlock lid for this recipe. Wash the jar and all the utensils you will be using in hot water or run them through a hot rinse cycle in the dishwasher.

Place the star anise and cloves in a small piece of muslin, tie into a bundle and set aside. Remove the outer leaves of the cabbage. Choose one of the outer leaves, wash it well and set aside. Shred the cabbage in a food processor, or slice by hand or use a mandoline, then place in a large glass or stainless steel bowl. Sprinkle on the salt, chopped dill and juniper berries, mix well, cover and set aside while you prepare the starter culture.

Dissolve the starter culture in water according to the packet instructions (the amount of water will depend on the brand you are using). Add to the cabbage along with the muslin bag containing the spices and mix well.

Fill the prepared jar with the cabbage, pressing down well with a large spoon or potato masher to remove any air pockets and leaving 2 cm of room free at the top. The cabbage should be completely submerged in the liquid; add more water if necessary.

Take the clean cabbage leaf, fold it up and place it on top of the cabbage mixture, then add a small glass weight (a shot glass is ideal) to keep everything submerged. Close the lid, then wrap a tea towel around the side of the jar to block out the light. Store in a dark place with a temperature of 16–23°C for 10–14 days. (Place the jar in an esky to maintain a more consistent temperature.) Different vegetables have different culturing times and the warmer it is the shorter the time needed. The longer you leave the jar, the higher the level of good bacteria present and the tangier the flavour.

Chill before eating. Once opened, mix through the dill tips and serve. The sauerkraut will last for up to 2 months in the fridge when kept submerged in the liquid. If unopened, it will keep for up to 9 months in the fridge.

Makes 1 x 1.5-litre jar

GLOSSARY

Activated nuts and seeds

Nuts are a great source of healthy fats, but they contain phytic acid, which when consumed binds to minerals such as iron, zinc, calcium, potassium and magnesium so that they can't be readily absorbed. Activating nuts and seeds lessens the phytates, making sure that we absorb as many of the good things as possible. Activated nuts and seeds are available from health food stores. Or to save money and make your own, simply soak the nuts in filtered water (hard nuts, like almonds, need to soak for 12 hours; softer nuts, like cashews and macadamias, only need 4–6 hours). Rinse the nuts under running water, then spread out on a baking tray and place in a 50°C oven or dehydrator to dry out. This will take anywhere from 6 to 24 hours, depending on the temperature. Store in an airtight container in the pantry for up to 3 months.

Apple cider vinegar

I use raw, organic apple cider vinegar, which is sometimes labelled 'apple cider vinegar with mother'. The 'mother' is made of enzymes and bacteria and has a cobweb-like appearance. Apple cider vinegar is rich in potassium and is believed to help clear up skin conditions. I love using it in dressings and stocks and often dilute some in warm water to make a great morning drink. Raw apple cider vinegar can be found at health food stores.

Arrowroot

Arrowroot is a starch made from the roots of several tropical plants. In Australia, arrowroot and tapioca flour are considered the same, even though they are actually from different plants. It can be found at health food stores and some supermarkets. *See also* Tapioca.

Banana flowers

Banana flowers are large, dark purple-red blossoms from banana trees, and can be eaten raw or cooked. The flowers grow on the end of a bunch of bananas, and the tender yellow-green leaves inside can be used in soups, stir-fries and salads. Banana flowers quickly go brown after the husks have been removed, so make sure you pop them in a bowl of water with some lemon juice or vinegar to prevent this. The flavour is a little bitter and they provide lovely crunch to any Asian-inspired salad. They are rich in Vitamin A, C and E, fibres, potassium and magnesium.

Bonito flakes

Bonito flakes are made from the bonito fish, which is like a small tuna. The fish is smoked, fermented, dried and shaved, and the end product looks similar to wood shavings. Bonito flakes are used to garnish Japanese dishes, to make sauces such as ponzu, soups such as miso and to make the Japanese stock, dashi. You can find bonito flakes in Asian food stores.

Cacao nibs

Cacao nibs are cacao beans that have been roasted, shelled and crushed. Cacao nibs have no added sugar or other nasties (unlike many processed cacao products), though they are still a stimulant so try not to have them in the evening. Cacao is one of the best sources of magnesium, as well as a good source of antioxidants, copper, zinc, iron and potassium. Cacao nibs are available from health food stores.

Capers and caper berries

Capers and caper berries come from a bush that is native to the Mediterranean. Capers are the unopened flower bud of the bush, while caper berries are the larger fruit. Both are usually pickled and sold in jars of brine. They are available from supermarkets and delicatessens.

Chia seeds

Chia seeds come from a Latin-American plant and they pack a huge punch when it comes to nutrients. They are an excellent source of protein and also contain omega-3 and omega-6 fatty acids, calcium, potassium, iron and magnesium. When placed in liquid, chia seeds swell to 17 times their original size, so they are a great substitute for traditional thickening agents like cornstarch. I love sprinkling chia seeds into smoothies, muesli, salads and desserts. You can buy them from health food stores and some supermarkets.

COCONUTS
Coconut aminos

Coconut aminos is made from the raw sap of the coconut tree, which is naturally aged and blended with sea salt. It is a great alternative to soy sauce as it has a higher amino acid content and no gluten. It is also slightly less salty than tamari. You'll find coconut aminos in health food stores.

Coconut oil

Coconut oil is extracted from the meat of matured coconuts. It has a high smoke point, making it great for cooking at high temperatures. The viscosity of coconut oil changes depending on the temperature and ranges from liquid to solid. Although coconut oil is high in saturated fats, they are mainly medium-chain saturated fatty acids, which means the body can use it quickly and does not have to store it. Coconut oil is available from supermarkets and health food stores. Look for virgin cold-pressed varieties as these have the least amount of processing.

Coconut sugar

Coconut sugar is produced from the sap of cut flower buds on the coconut palm and is subtly sweet with a caramel flavour. It is a good alternative to refined cane sugar as it has a lower GI (glycemic index) and a high mineral content. Like all sweeteners, I use coconut sugar sparingly. You will find it at health food stores and some supermarkets.

Young coconuts

Young coconuts are harvested at around 5–7 months and are usually white in colour. The best way to open one is to cut a circle in the top using a large knife and then prise this circle off. The amount of coconut water inside varies, but is usually around 250 ml. It is a good source of potassium and makes a refreshing drink on a hot day. Once you've poured the water out of the coconut, you can scoop out the soft flesh using a spoon. Look for young coconuts at Asian food stores and health food stores.

Daikon

Daikon, or Japanese radish, is a large, white radish that is commonly used in Japanese, Korean and South East Asian cuisines. It has a wide variety of uses – it is pickled, grated into sauces, simmered in broths and even stir-fried. Daikon is low in calories and contains high levels of vitamin C. It can be found at Asian grocers and some supermarkets.

Eggs

The best eggs come from free-range chickens, which are allowed to roam freely outside in the sunshine, eat insects and plants, and have a far healthier and happier life than ones trapped in cages. Free-range eggs taste better, have stronger shells, are less runny, and have firmer and brighter yolks. They also contain less cholesterol and saturated fat than caged eggs, and have higher levels of vitamin A, E and D, protein, beta-carotene and omega-3 fatty acids. I use extra-large eggs in my recipes.

Flaxseeds

Also known as linseeds, flaxseeds are one of the most concentrated plant sources of omega-3 fats. They can be ground up into flaxseed meal and are also used to create oil. Care needs to be taken in the storage of flaxseed products as they contain unsaturated fat and can go rancid if they aren't stored in an airtight container in a cool place. It is hard to absorb the nutrients in whole flaxseeds as they have a hard outer shell, so for maximum nutrition, it is best to consume them in ground or oil form. Flaxseed meal or oil can be added to muffins, muesli or smoothies for a fibre, antioxidant and omega-3 boost. Flaxseed products can be found at health food stores, as well as some supermarkets and pharmacies.

Galangal

Galangal is similar in appearance to ginger and has been used in Thai cooking for more than a thousand years. It is available in Asian supermarkets and some regular supermarkets, and is believed to relieve indigestion, flatulence, nausea and hiccups. It is fantastic in many kinds of Asian dishes, especially curries.

Goji berries

Goji berries are mainly grown in China, Mongolia and Tibet. They are bright pink and have a mild, tangy taste that is slightly sweet and sour. Goji berries are usually sold in dried form and have the same kind of shape and chewy texture as raisins. They contain all the essential amino acids and have the highest concentration of protein of any fruit. They also contain vitamin C, carotenoids, fibre, iron, calcium, zinc, selenium and many other important trace minerals. Goji berries are great for adding to muesli, desserts, sweet sauces and puddings. Goji berry powder is also available and can be stirred directly into juices, herbal teas, coconut water or plain water. Goji berries can be found at your local supermarket or health food store.

Good-quality fats

I use either coconut oil or good-quality animal fats for cooking as they have high smoke points (meaning they do not oxidise at high temperatures). Some of my favourite animal fats to use are lard (pork fat), tallow (rendered beef fat), rendered chicken fat and duck fat. These may be hard to find – ask at your local butcher or meat supplier, or you can also look online for meat suppliers who sell them. Extra-virgin olive oil is fantastic for salad dressings or for drizzling over finished dishes.

Hemp seeds

Hemp seeds come from the Cannabis plant, and while the hemp plant is in the same family as marijuana, the two plants are quite different: hemp seeds contain no or miniscule amounts of THC, the psychoactive substance found in marijuana. Hulled hemp seeds (the whole seed without the mineral rich outer shell) can be eaten raw, ground, sprouted, as hemp milk, prepared as tea and used in baking. Hemp seeds are a high-protein food source (with twice the amount of protein compared to chia seeds) and contain omega-3, omega-6 and 20 different varieties of amino acids, including all nine of the essential amino acids. You'll find hemp seeds at health food stores.

Maca powder

Maca is a rainforest herb that is high in protein and other nutrients. It is believed to increase energy and support the immune system. Try adding a spoonful of maca powder to your smoothies for a protein boost.

Meat

I always source the absolute best quality meat I can find – organic, pasture-raised beef and pork, and organic, free-range chicken. It really is worth paying a little extra for, as you know that the quality of the protein is second to none, that the animals have led happy lives and haven't been injected full of hormones and antibiotics and that the flavour will always be amazing. If you don't have a good butcher near you, there are lots of online stores that will deliver to your door.

Nori sheets

Nori is a dark green, paper-like, toasted seaweed used for most kinds of sushi and other Japanese dishes. Nori provides an abundance of essential nutrients and is rich in vitamins, iron, minerals, amino acids, omega-3 and omega-6, and anti-oxidants. Nori sheets are commonly used to roll sushi, but they can also be added to salads, soups, and fish, meat and vegetable dishes. You can buy nori sheets from Asian grocers and most supermarkets.

Psyllium husks and psyllium seed powder

Psyllium, also known as ispaghula, is a gluten free, light brown soluble fibre produced from the Plantago ovata plant, native to India and Pakistan. Psyllium is an indigestible dietary fibre, and is primarily used to maintain intestinal health, as the high fibre content absorbs excess liquid in the gut. When exposed to liquids, the husks swell up to create a gel. It is therefore important to drink plenty of fluids when consuming psyllium. Psyllium products can be found at health food stores and some supermarkets.

Salt

I like to use sea salt or Himalayan salt in my cooking, as they are less processed than table salt, contain more minerals and have a lovely crunchy texture. Himalayan salt is light pink in colour due to the presence of a number of different minerals, including iron, magnesium, calcium and copper. You can purchase both sea salt and Himalayan salt at supermarkets and health food stores.

Shiso leaves

Shiso leaves, also known as perilla, are commonly used in Japanese cuisine. There are red, purple and green varieties of shiso leaf and they are used in many ways – finely sliced on top of noodle dishes, chopped and added to batters, in tempura, or scattered over any number of dishes as a garnish. Shiso has quite a pungent, grassy flavour that is lost when it is cooked for a long time. You can find shiso leaves at Asian grocers.

Shrimp paste (belacan)

Shrimp paste is used in many different Asian cuisines and is an essential ingredient in numerous curries and sauces. It is made from tiny shrimp mixed with salt and fermented, then ground into a smooth paste and sun dried. Shrimp paste has quite a powerful smell and taste, so should only be used in small quantities. You can find it in Asian grocers and some supermarkets.

Sumac

Sumac is a spice made from red sumac berries that have been dried and crushed. It has antimicrobial properties and a tangy, lemony flavour, which makes it ideal for pairing with seafood. It's also delicious in salad dressings.

Tamarind

Tamarind juice or pulp is made from the pods of the tamarind tree and is used as a souring agent, particularly in Indian dishes, chutneys and curries. It is also used as an ingredient in sauces and side dishes for pork, chicken and fish. It can be found at Asian grocers and some supermarkets.

Tapioca flour

Tapioca flour is made by grinding up the dried root of the manioc (also known as cassava) plant. It can be used to thicken dishes or in gluten-free baking. You can find tapioca flour at health food stores and some supermarkets. *See also* Arrowroot.

Wakame

Wakame is an edible seaweed commonly used in Japanese, Korean and Chinese cuisine. It is great in soups, salads and stir-fries. Wakame contains iron, magnesium, iodine, calcium and lignans. You can find it in Asian grocers and some supermarkets.

Yuzu juice

Yuzu is a Japanese citrus fruit that has an extraordinary spicy citrus flavour, somewhere between a lemon and a lime. Yuzu juice is very high in vitamin C and is great in cocktails, dressings, dips and sashimi dishes. You can buy yuzu juice from Asian grocers.

THANK YOU

Thank you to my beautiful partner in life and love, Nicola. I am seriously the luckiest bloke on the planet. Thank you for nurturing me and the little bunnies, Indii and Chilli, with love and food. I love you!

To my bunnies, Indii and Chilli – you know this book wouldn't have come about if it weren't for you. I love you both so much and you are both so unique in your own special ways. I hope that by the time your own children are at school this way of living will be considered normal and the current dietary guidelines considered extreme.

To Mark Roper (photography) and Deb Kaloper (styling) – thanks for once again making my food shine brightly!

To Ben Dearnley (photography) and Emma Knowles (styling) – thanks for the extra lifestyle images for the book.

To Jason Loucas (photography) and Vivien Walsh (styling) – thanks for the fantastic cover shots.

To Mary Small – once again, it was a pleasure working with you and creating another much needed book.

To Jane Winning – thanks once again for making sure all my recipes are tested for everyone cooking from the book.

To Megan Johnston – thank you for your careful and thorough editing.

To Kirby Armstrong – thanks again for creating another fabulous design for the book.

To Northwood Green – thanks for your brilliant cover design.

To Monica and Jacinta Cannataci – girls, I can't thank you enough and I am so happy that you have discovered that food really is medicine. You are the doctors of the future.

To Charlotte Ree – thanks for being the best publicist any author could wish to work with.

To Mum – thanks for passing on your love of cooking.

And finally to my mentors and the trailblazers in health and nutrition, I couldn't have done it without you: Nora Gedgaudas and Lisa Collins, Dr Libby, Trevor Hendy, Luke Hines, Helen Padarin, Pete Melov, Rudy Eckhardt, Pete Bablis, William (Bill) Davis, Tim Noakes, Gary Fettke, David Perlmutter, Gary Taubes, Frank Lipman, Wes and Charlotte Carr, Nahko Bear, Michael Franti, Trevor Hall, David Gillespie, Ben Balzer, Loren Cordain, Bruce Fife, Mat Lalonde, Martha Herbert, Joseph Mercola, Sally Fallon, Dr Natasha Campbell-McBride, Kitsa Yanniotis and Donna Gates.

Cook with Love & Laughter

Pete Evans

INDEX

A

Aioli 242
almond butter 58
Andouille sausages with
poached egg and
asparagus 30
Apple and berry crumble 234
artichoke tartare sauce 132
Asian ceviche salad 92
Asian slaw 68
asparagus
Andouille sausages with
poached egg and
asparagus 30
Shaved asparagus salad with
green goddess dressing 70
avocado
avocado dip 59
Avocado fries 82
avocado green salad 162
avocado salad 203
Chicken, avocado and
cauliflower sushi 46
guacamole 49, 52

B

bacon
Bacon and sherry
vinaigrette 250
Manu's baby leeks with
soft-boiled egg and truffled
bacon and sherry
vinaigrette 89
Roasted broccoli and
bacon 211
balsamic dressing 73
Banana flower salad with
crackling chicken 104
Banana muffins 226
barbecue ideas
balsamic zucchini 143
best beef cuts 143
grilled sardines 145
lamb skewers 142

marinades 143
spice rub for meat 142
stuffed mushrooms 142
Barbecued balsamic
veggies 220
Barbecued fish with fennel,
zucchini and currants 152
Barbecued Moroccan
flounder 159
Barbecued steak with
chimichurri 198
beef
Beef bone broth 254
Beef carpaccio with celeriac
remoulade 122
Beef heart salad 118
best barbecue cuts 143
Burger with the lot 140
Japanese beef tataki 197
spicy Mexican beef 52
Thai beef salad 116
see also steak
beef liver, spiced, with
avocado salad 203
beetroot
Beetroot chimichurri 251
Beetroot harissa 244
Chocolate and beetroot mud
cakes 238
Raw beetroot salad 81
boiled eggs with salmon roe 29
Bok choy with ginger 214
bone broth 24, 51, 254
bone marrow, roasted, with
scrambled eggs 35
Brazilian fish stew 154
bread 65, 138
Coconut pita breads 257
Nic's paleo bread 257
paleo bread 65, 138, 172
paleo bread with toppings 29
Seed and nut bread 256
broccoli 131
broccoli rice 208
Broccoli soup with wild
trout 131

Broccoli stem stir-fry 218
Broccoli tabbouli 206
Roasted broccoli and
bacon 211
Burger with the lot 140

C

cabbage 110
Asian ceviche salad 92
Asian slaw 68
Sauerkraut with dill and
juniper berries 258
Shredded cabbage salad with
walnuts and speck 110
Cajun spice mix 203
cakes
Banana muffins 226
Chocolate and beetroot mud
cakes 238
Chocolate brownies 232
Coconut macaroons 224
Cashew cheese 256
cauliflower
cauliflower grits 151
cauliflower rice 208
Chicken, avocado and
cauliflower sushi 46
Indian cauliflower rice 212
pizza base 185
Quick fish curry with roasted
cauliflower 166
celeriac
celeriac remoulade 122
Chicken and celeriac
sandwiches with avocado
and sauerkraut 65
Fennel and celeriac salad
with walnut and
mustard dressing 76
celery and nut cheese 48
ceviche 172
Ceviche with pomegranate and
mango 102
'Cherry Ripe' bites 237
Chia bircher 21, 28

chicken
    Banana flower salad with
        crackling chicken 104
    Chicken, avocado and
        cauliflower sushi 46
    Chicken and celeriac
        sandwiches with avocado
        and sauerkraut 65
    Chicken waldorf salad 109
    Crackling chicken 180
    Indian-style roast chicken
        drumsticks 174
    Paleo club sanga 138
    Piri-piri chicken skewers 192
    Pistachio-crusted chicken
        with spicy aioli 176
    Thai chicken cakes 57
    Yakitori chicken skewers 179
    Chicken liver nuggets 60
    chicken liver pâté 173
chillies
    Beetroot harissa 244
    Grilled sardines with chilli,
        oregano and lemon 145
    Roasted green chillies with
        romesco sauce 217
Chimichurri 198, 251
Chocolate and beetroot mud
    cakes 238
Chocolate brownies 232
coconut dressing 84
Coconut macaroons 224
Coconut pita breads 257
coriander dressing 92
Crackling chicken 180
Crumbed fish burgers with
    artichoke tartare sauce 132
curry
    Curried egg omelette 38
    curry sauce 186
    Jamaican mussel and clam
        curry 168
    Quick fish curry with roasted
        cauliflower 166

D
dairy-free pesto 59
desserts
    Apple and berry crumble 234
    'Cherry Ripe' bites 237
    see also cakes

digestif 230
dips
    avocado dip 59
    dairy-free pesto 59
    guacamole 49
    mint yoghurt 191
    nut cheese 48
    Olive tapenade 247
    tzatziki 51
dressings
    Aioli 242
    Asian dressing 68
    Bacon and sherry
        vinaigrette 250
    balsamic dressing 73
    coconut dressing 84
    coriander dressing 92
    Green goddess dressing 70,
        250
    harissa and preserved lemon
        aioli 96
    herb aioli 60
    Herb and anchovy
        dressing 253
    Herb and garlic
        vinaigrette 252
    herb ranch dressing 109
    lemon dressing 113
    Mayonnaise 242
    mustard and honey
        dressing 90
    Mustard vinaigrette 252
    Nam jim dressing 253
    orange and walnut
        dressing 86
    spicy aioli 176
    tataki dressing 197
    walnut and mustard
        dressing 76
    zingy Italian dressing 86
    see also sauces
drinks
    digestif 230
    ginseng tea 231
    hazelnut milk, warm 231
    herbal drink 230
    hot chocolate 230
    macadamia milk, warm 231
    Sunshine mylk 16
duck, crackling 180
dukkah 87

E
Eggplant and prawn mini
    pizzas 54
eggs
    Andouille sausages with
        poached egg and
        asparagus 30
    boiled eggs with salmon
        roe 29
    Curried egg omelette 38
    egg sauce 182
    Green eggs and ham 44
        hard-boiled eggs with
        mayonnaise and
        herbs 48
    hard-boiled eggs as snacks 49
    Manu's baby leeks with
        soft-boiled egg and
        truffled bacon and
        sherry vinaigrette 89
    Nom Nom's egg foo
        young-ish 62
    Perfect steak and eggs with
        kale and almonds 41
    Raw beetroot salad 81
    Scrambled eggs with roasted
        bone marrow 35
    scrambled eggs on toast with
        smoked salmon 28
    Scrambled eggs with zucchini
        spaghetti and raisins 22
    Simple caesar salad 106
    Soft-boiled duck eggs with
        sautéed greens and
        olive tapenade 36
    Thai pork mince with fried
        egg 27

F
Fattoush with prawns 101
fennel
    Barbecued fish with fennel,
        zucchini and currants
        152
    Fennel and celeriac
        salad with walnut and
        mustard dressing 76
    Fennel sausages with onion
        gravy 194

Salmon, fennel and watercress salad 90
Squid salad with fennel and burnt lemon 98
fermented vegetables 51, 68
figs: Prosciutto with fig and radish 113
fish *see* seafood
Fresh cos salad with mustard vinaigrette 74
Fresh veggie and tzatziki sandwich 51
frittata 29

G

gazpacho 172
ginger, honey and tamari marinade 143
ginseng tea 231
Gozleme of lamb, mint and spinach 191
Greek marinade 143
Green eggs and ham 44
Green goddess dressing 70, 250
Grilled sardines with chilli, oregano and lemon 145
guacamole 49, 52
Gypsy salad 84

H

ham
Green eggs and ham 44
iceberg lettuce and ham salad wraps 49
Nom Nom's egg foo young-ish 62
hard-boiled eggs with mayonnaise and herbs 48
harissa and preserved lemon aioli 96
hazelnut milk, warm 231
herb aioli 60
Herb and anchovy dressing 253
Herb and garlic vinaigrette 252
herb ranch dressing 109
herbal drink 230
herbs 87, 230
hot chocolate 230
Hot and sour soup 128

I

iceberg lettuce and ham salad wraps 49
Indian cauliflower rice 212
Indian spice marinade 174
Indian-style roast chicken drumsticks 174

J

Jamaican mussel and clam curry 168
Japanese beef tataki 197
Japanese tuna salad 95
jerk spice 146

K

kale chips 173
kebabs *see* skewers
Korean bulgogi marinade 143
Korean steak tartare with kimchi and nashi 121

L

lamb
Gozleme of lamb, mint and spinach 191
lamb skewers 142
leeks: Manu's baby leeks with soft-boiled egg and truffled bacon and sherry vinaigrette 89
leftovers 29
lemon dressing 113
lettuce
Fresh cos salad with mustard vinaigrette 74
iceberg lettuce and ham salad wraps 49
Lyonnaise salad with pork scratchings 114
Simple caesar salad 106
Lyonnaise salad with pork scratchings 114

M

Macadamia cheese 256
macadamia milk, warm 231
macadamia satay sauce 188

Manu's baby leeks with soft-boiled egg and truffled bacon and sherry vinaigrette 89
Mayonnaise 242
Mexican fajita marinade 143
mince
Paleo nachos 52
Spaghetti and meatballs 200
Thai pork mince with fried egg 27
mint yoghurt 191
mud cakes, chocolate and beetroot 238
mushrooms, stuffed 142
Mussel moolie 160
mustard and honey dressing 90
Mustard vinaigrette 252
My steak sanga 134

N

Nam jim dressing 253
Nic's paleo bread 257
Nom Nom's egg foo young-ish 62
Nourishing broth with marrow and herbs 24
nuoc cham 32
nut butters 58
nut cheeses 59, 256

O

offal 118
Beef heart salad 118
Spiced beef liver with avocado salad 203
olives
Fish with tomato, olives and caper berries 165
Olive tapenade 247
omelette, curried egg 38
onion ponzu 197
orange and walnut dressing 86

P

paleo bread 65, 138, 172
Nic's paleo bread 257
with toppings 29
Paleo buns 248
Paleo club sanga 138

Paleo nachos 52
paleo sushi 46
pancakes, Vietnamese, with prawn and pork salad 32
parsnip noodles 200
Perfect prawn salad 96
Perfect steak and eggs with kale and almonds 41
pesto, dairy-free 59
Piri-piri chicken skewers 192
Pistachio-crusted chicken with spicy aioli 176
pizzas
Eggplant and prawn mini pizzas 54
Prosciutto pizza 185
Pomegranate and coconut popsicles 229
pork
Fennel sausages with onion gravy 194
Hot and sour soup 128
Pork katsu with curry sauce 186
pork scratchings 114
Satay pork skewers 188
Vietnamese pancakes with prawn and pork salad 32
prawns
Eggplant and prawn mini pizzas 54
Fattoush with prawns 101
Perfect prawn salad 96
Prawn rolls 137
Prawns and grits 151
quick prawn dish 173
Vietnamese pancakes with prawn and pork salad 32
Prosciutto with fig and radish 113
Prosciutto pizza 185
pumpkin seed spread 58

Q

Quick fish curry with roasted cauliflower 166

R

Raw beetroot salad 81
roast meat leftovers 29

Roasted broccoli and bacon 211
Roasted green chillies with romesco sauce 217
Roasted trout with jerk spice glaze 146
Rocket and pear salad with balsamic dressing 73
romesco sauce 217

S

salad leaves
dressing 86
drying 87
salads
Asian ceviche salad 92
Asian slaw 68
avocado green salad 162
avocado salad 203
Banana flower salad with crackling chicken 104
Beef heart salad 118
Broccoli tabbouli 206
Chicken waldorf salad 109
Fattoush with prawns 101
Fennel and celeriac salad with walnut and mustard dressing 76
Fresh cos salad with mustard vinaigrette 74
Gypsy salad 84
Japanese tuna salad 95
Lyonnaise salad with pork scratchings 114
Manu's baby leeks with soft-boiled egg and truffled bacon and sherry vinaigrette 89
Perfect prawn salad 96
Raw beetroot salad 81
Rocket and pear salad with balsamic dressing 73
Salmon, fennel and watercress salad 90
Salsa verde 255
Shaved asparagus salad with green goddess dressing 70
Shredded cabbage salad with walnuts and speck 110

Simple caesar salad 106
Squid salad with fennel and burnt lemon 98
Thai beef salad 116
Salmon, fennel and watercress salad 90
salmon roe 90
Salsa verde 255
sandwiches
Burger with the lot 140
Chicken and celeriac sandwiches with avocado and sauerkraut 65
Fresh veggie and tzatziki sandwich 51
My steak sanga 134
Paleo club sanga 138
Prawn rolls 137
sardines, grilled, with chilli, oregano and lemon 145
sashimi 197
Satay pork skewers 188
sauces
artichoke tartare sauce 132
curry sauce 186
egg sauce 182
macadamia satay sauce 188
piri-piri sauce 192
romesco sauce 217
tomato sauce 200
see also dressings
Sauerkraut with dill and juniper berries 258
sausages 30, 194
Andouille sausages with poached egg and asparagus 30
Fennel sausages with onion gravy 194
Scrambled eggs with roasted bone marrow 35
Scrambled eggs on toast with smoked salmon 28
Scrambled eggs with zucchini spaghetti and raisins 22
seafood
Asian ceviche salad 92
Barbecued fish with fennel, zucchini and currants 152
Barbecued Moroccan flounder 159

Brazilian fish stew 154
Broccoli soup with wild trout 131
Ceviche with pomegranate and mango 102
Crumbed fish burgers with artichoke tartare sauce 132
fish in crazy water 171
fish stock 154, 159
Fish with tomato, olives and caper berries 165
Fish wings 'osso buco' 148
Grilled sardines with chilli, oregano and lemon 145
Jamaican mussel and clam curry 168
Japanese tuna salad 95
Mussel moolie 160
Quick fish curry with roasted cauliflower 166
Roasted trout with jerk spice glaze 146
Snapper acqua pazza 171
Spicy fish soup 126
Squid salad with fennel and burnt lemon 98
Taj and Johnny's fish and chips 162
see also prawns
seed butters 58
Seed and nut bread 256
seeds 87
shallots, crispy 104
Shaved asparagus salad with green goddess dressing 70
Shredded cabbage salad with walnuts and speck 110
Simple caesar salad 106
skewers
Piri-piri chicken skewers 192
Satay pork skewers 188
Yakitori chicken skewers 179
Snapper acqua pazza (fish in crazy water) 171
Soft-boiled duck eggs with sautéed greens and olive tapenade 36
soup
Beef bone broth 254
for breakfast 28, 151

Broccoli soup with wild trout 131
gazpacho 172
Hot and sour soup 128
Nourishing broth with marrow and herbs 24
Spicy fish soup 126
Spaghetti and meatballs 200
spice rub 142
Spiced beef liver with avocado salad 203
spices 168
spicy aioli 176
Spicy fish soup 126
spinach
Gozleme of lamb, mint and spinach 191
Nom Nom's egg foo young-ish 62
spreads 58–9
Squid salad with fennel and burnt lemon 98
steak
Barbecued steak with chimichurri 198
Japanese beef tataki 197
Korean steak tartare wuth kimchi and nashi 121
My steak sanga 134
Perfect steak and eggs with kale and almonds 41
stir-fry, broccoli stem 218
stock 126
Sunshine mylk 16
Superfood 'cereal' 18, 28
sushi, chicken, avocado and cauliflower 46

T

Taj and Johnny's fish and chips 162
tapenade 36
tataki dressing 197
teriyaki marinade 143
Thai beef salad 116
Thai chicken cakes 57
Thai pork mince with fried egg 27
tomatoes
gazpacho 172
romesco sauce 217

Snapper acqua pazza (fish in crazy water) 171
Tomato relish 255
tomato salsa 52
tomato sauce 200
trout, roasted, with jerk spice glaze 146
tzatziki 51

V

vegetables
Barbecued balsamic veggies 220
Fresh veggie and tzatziki sandwich 51
Vietnamese pancakes with prawn and pork salad 32

W

walnut and mustard dressing 76

Y

Yakitori chicken skewers 179

Z

zingy Italian dressing 86
zucchini
balsamic zucchini 143
Barbecued fish with fennel, zucchini and currants 152
Zucchini carbonara 182
Zucchini rice 208
zucchini spaghetti 22

A PLUM BOOK

First published in 2015 by
Pan Macmillan Australia Pty Limited
Level 25, 1 Market Street,
Sydney, NSW 2000, Australia

Level 1, 15–19 Claremont Street,
South Yarra, Victoria 3141, Australia

Design by Kirby Armstrong
Cover design by Northwood Green
Photography by Mark Roper (with additional photography by Ben Dearnley, Jason Loucas, Steve Brown and Anson Smart)
Prop and food styling by Deb Kaloper (with additional styling by Emma Knowles, Vivien Walsh and David Morgan)
Edited by Megan Johnston
Typeset by Pauline Haas
Index by Jo Rudd
Colour reproduction by Splitting Image Colour Studio
Printed and bound in China by 1010 Printing International Limited

A CIP catalogue record for this book is available from the National Library of Australia.

10 9 8 7 6 5 4 3 2

Visit What Should I Eat? to find recipes from this book and lots more.
whatshouldieat.com.au
instagram.com/whatshouldieat.com.au